NOW THAT WE HAVE
ALL THESE PEOPLE,
WHAT ARE WE SUPPOSED
TO DO WITH THEM?

A Field Guide To Workforce Optimization

by
Ken Johnson

ISBN: 1-4196-9167-8
ISBN-13: 9781419691676

Visit www.booksurge.com to order additional copies.

Table Of Contents

Author's Preface: Why Bother Trying Workforce Optimization?

My Offer To You

Think of this as a recipe for something great! Ok, a really long recipe, but still, it's for something great. This book not only explains the theory of the science of Workforce Optimization, but it also outlines the practical steps to take should you want to implement the theory at your company. You'll also find included herewith instructions (see Appendix Six) on how to secure, at no additional cost, the PC version of our proprietary computer software program, **_P.E.R.F.O.R.M._**, that will enable your implementation. My offer to you, simply put, is that if you apply this recipe, you'll be able to serve something great for your company: you'll be able to lead the transformation that capitalizes on what is truly your company's greatest asset – **your people!** You will be part of the effort that enables your company's workforce to achieve to its highest possible potential. You'll be able to implement Workforce Optimization!

Let's start off right up front with a healthy, honest, "cut to the chase" agreement of what we're looking at when I use the phrase "Workforce Optimization." What is it that businesses want? Results. Financial results. There's nothing wrong or evil in that goal, it's the inherent goal of a viable organization. A company may choose to do something supremely noble with its profit, like sponsor efforts to find a cure for cancer or world hunger, and many do, or it may choose to simply make a profit so it can pay its employees and they can all enjoy a better quality of life. What a company does with its profit is another thing altogether, but it all begins with achieving results. Financial results.

So the company looks to its leaders to strategize and lead it in a direction that is profitable. The leaders then turn to their managers, and they, in turn, rely on the bulk of the workforce, the employees, to do the things that make the company operate, and hopefully, at the end of it all, profitable. No matter how you look at it: **it all comes down to your people.**

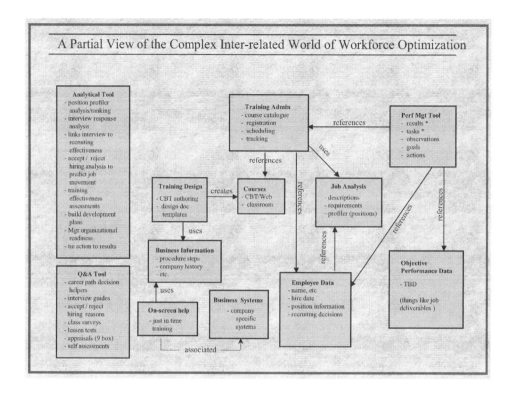

A Partial View of the Complex Inter-related World of Workforce Optimization

And what do you think of when you think of the people element of running a business? The Human Resources Department! But if we are to truly optimize the efforts of our workforce, we have to take a larger view of what it typically means to manage the "human resource," and what we can do to "optimize" the efforts of the human resources professionals. So let's start out by considering the payoff if we agree that Human Resources Management is bigger than just benefits and payroll. Since the success of all businesses is a matter of how well it's employees work, the true role of Human Resources Management is to help the company make the most of its employees' **job performance**. Benefits and payroll are necessary, even vital, components of any company, and their effect on an employee's job performance cannot be underestimated, but they are only one small piece of a rather large and complex matrix that comprises all of what a company can do to affect the performance of its workforce. We in the HR group need to be prepared to help the company in any way available to positively affect employee job performance. **Any** way available! And the smartest approach, with the greatest potential to positively affect business results is to manage both the forest and the trees. This is the heart of Workforce Optimization!

I'll admit that I'm a bit nervous that, after reading the recipe even for just a short while, I'll be like a magician who's told someone the secret to the prestige. After you know how to do the magic trick it loses all of its impact. That's ok, I'm not really that concerned with your being impressed with me. All I'm hoping for is to have helped in some way those of us who collectively specialize in the science and art of supporting business and industry in its work with its employees, to find better and better ways to boost employee engagement and satisfaction. That's all. Just a simple, easy little thing.

Interested? Even just a little bit? Then jump in, the train's about to take off!

Chapter One:
The 30,000 ft. View

- Workforce Optimization Is A Profit Center

- Results Oriented: Higher Job Performance

- Results Oriented: Faster Time-To-Performance

Workforce Optimization Is A Profit Center

Start to think of working with the workforce of a company for what it truly is: a profit center. Like any good profit center manager, those who manage the areas of a company that affect the job performance of the workforce are really looking to maximize return on investment (ROI.) When we talk about how this translates into optimizing the workforce, I'm referring to the concept of getting more job results out of the people you have to work with. If this were a Financial Analysis course, I'd refer to it as one of the Efficiency Ratios. If we can get higher performance from the same number of people or faster time for a new person to reach a level where he/she is fully performing, both through the techniques explained in this book, then the company is more profitable.

These, then, are the two basic ways in which Workforce Optimization contributes as a profit center:
- Higher performance results;
    - more output from the same number of people;
    - the same output from fewer people;
    - more output from fewer people;
- Faster "time-to-performance".

I'll explain each in just a moment, but first realize that we need to fully understand what "results" means, and we also will need to know, once we know what "results" mean, how to get people to achieve those results. The majority of this book is an attempt to explain how things done with the workforce will contribute to higher results. "Results" in terms of how to identify what results you should expect, how to measure their achievement, and how to raise the bar on them. For a quick definition of what "results" are, think of the clue you've already read. When I say "results" what I mean is higher job performance, which leads directly to **higher job output**, which leads directly to **higher financial results** for the company. Once we know, from the business' perspective, what "higher" is, then we can apply the techniques throughout this book to get the workforce to "higher." Essentially, it's through better techniques for recruiting, hiring, developing, rewarding, and even terminating, but there's plenty more to discuss on those subjects later in the book . . .

A Quick Fix: Workforce Optimization Defined

If we're going to consider the two areas of payoff (higher performance and faster time-to-performance) for undertaking this workforce optimization journey, then we're going to need a quick fix for a definition of what the term "workforce optimization" means. Everyone likes a succinct relating of a concept they're trying to master, so I'm sure you're already looking for a working definition of the term so that you can begin to attach broader and deeper meaning to the skeleton of understanding. To get us off to a good start, let me offer this quick, summary, high-level working definition of what is meant by the term "workforce optimization." Workforce optimization is the management practice of influencing events and environment so that individuals and the collective employee workforce achieve(s) to their/its maximum potential. The events and environment influenced are both single areas of involvement, but, even more importantly, management of **the combined effect of multiple factors** on individual and collective job task performance.

Ok, now we're ready to explore the ways in which workforce optimization operates as a profit center . . .

Higher Performance Results Explained

When a group of people is doing a job, let's say making widgets, there are standard ways to perform the tasks of the job that result in widgets. Clever manufacturing departments will tell you what is the average number of widgets per person per hour, and when to expect peaks and valleys in that output. For example, let's say that 50 people can produce an average of 200 widgets per hour, that's an average of 4 widgets per person per hour (I like to make the math easy in these examples!)

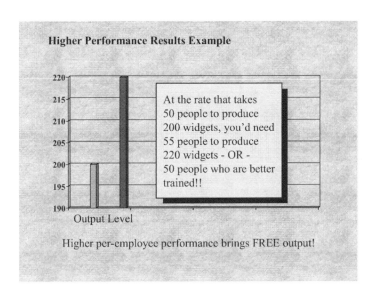

Higher Performance Results Example

At the rate that takes 50 people to produce 200 widgets, you'd need 55 people to produce 220 widgets - OR - 50 people who are better trained!!

Output Level

Higher per-employee performance brings FREE output!

Now, in come the experts in tinkering with the people aspect of the company, the Workforce Optimization practitioners. They begin to study the job, not just time and motion, although that's a great place to look, but also motivation, backgrounds of top performers, and all sorts of things explained here in our recipe book. Through intervention, these professionals identify techniques for working with the employees which result in a 10% boost in **job results** (notice I carefully avoided writing "job <u>performance</u>" because what really matters is **not** the job performance, but rather what effect did that have on the results delivered!) Now instead of those 50 people turning out 200 widgets per hour, they can collectively produce 220 widgets per hour, or an increase equal to adding 5 new people if they all produced at the old level. It's like getting **free output** just for finding better ways to engage the workforce in their job!!

But how do you know what kind of performance to expect? One of the great outcomes of Workforce Optimization movement is the discovery of theories and methodology to **boost total workforce output** by understanding and replicating the successes of the company's **top ten percent performers**. There's something about a champion that makes a person a champion. If you put them in a quagmire with the rest of the group, they'll always come out on top. It's not a bad thing, it's a factor of the human experience. Some people have the spirit of a champion and some don't. Some people have it, and it takes a good coach to help them realize it and apply it to its fullest potential! What the "champion spirit" tells us is that those who lead your workforce will always lead your workforce, but they also help you understand what others could do to become more like a champion. We'll explore this more later, but here are some techniques you'll want to keep in mind:

- invest in your top performers – help them get higher;
- help everyone, but invest in your top performers;
- dissect the background and habits of your top performers so you know how to advise others;
- compare top performers as a peer group, and let them challenge themselves higher – you can **manage to potential** (no limits!) not expectation (goals & standards)!

- - - CAUTION!!! - - -   Some people only **appear** to be champions because they're at the top, while their path to the top is strewn with those whom they've abused and stood on in order to reach higher. These are merely the "pigs at the trough." They will eventually undo themselves. One element of dissecting the top performers is to make sure we look at "how" without wearing rose-colored glasses (I won't say "put on your cynical glasses", although that might not be a bad idea . . .) before jumping to conclusions. We want to repeat what leads to top performance without compromising teamwork.

Faster "Time-To-Performance' Explained

I love to talk about this aspect! Consider a company's Sales force. These are the people who lead the charge into the marketplace. Much like the manufacturing arm of the company, the people who manage the Sales area also keep strict records on the work level of their employees too. Replacing "widgets per person per hour" with measurements such as "sales calls per week or month", "revenue per customer per month", "number and mix of products purchased per customer per month", etc. These gauge the "outputs" of the Sales function in the company, and there are minimum acceptable levels of performance against them.

So, now along comes those same sharp practitioners of Workforce Optimization, and now they're looking at how we can optimize the job efforts of the Sales team. Let's just say that before they arrive it takes the average new Sales person

18 months before he or she is performing at a level that is m

acceptable levels of performance, which, for the revenue m

level is $10,000 per month. If we grant 6 months grace p

to secure his/her first $2,000 per month, with the old

reaching $10,000 per month at the 18 month anniv﹍

average of **.15%** month over month aggregate growth.

	18 Months to Goal	15 Months to Goal
Month 6	$2,000	$2,000
Month 7	$2,300	$2,400
Month 8	$2,645	$2,880
Month 9	$3,042	$3,456
Month 10	$3,498	$4,147
Month 11	$4,023	$4,977
Month 12	$4,626	$5,972
Month 13	$5,320	$7,166
Month 14	$6,118	$8,600
Month 15	$7,036	$10,320
Month 16	$8,091	$12,383
Month 17	$9,305	$14,860
Month 18	$10,701	$17,832
Total	**$68,704**	**$96,993**

Now let's fast-forward and assume that, as a result of investigation and analysis, working together the Sales team and the Workforce Optimization people identify ways top performers do things, and how they got to be top performers, and they begin to use that insight to better recruit and develop new Sales people. If the effect of this new program results in a new Sales person reaching the minimum acceptable level of performance sooner (same $10,000 level) then the new program has actually **netted the company the growth in revenue** from that employee that represents how much he/she would have made at the old "up to speed" rate of 18 months compared to the new "up to speed" rate. If the new "up to speed" rate is 15 months, which is a growth rate of **.02%** month

month, then the resulting **in the bank** higher revenue for the company, for initial 18 month period, would be approximately **$28,289 more** per new sales person hired. One could even make a case that future sales results would be higher too, based on better skill sets, but that's more than I want to tackle here. You may have noticed that the grid started at month six instead of month one. That's because the first five months are dedicated to learning the right techniques without pressure for results. That may or may not be appropriate depending on what "time-to-performance" job you're working with. What's important is that we're comparing apples to apples, both start at month six and track to month 18, the only difference is the rate at which revenue is secured **due to better sales techniques**, or perhaps better recruiting because you now know better what type of person achieves the results you're after. This is what is meant when I referred to Workforce Optimization as being a profit center - **the company brings in higher revenue** because Workforce Optimization techniques help new people achieve faster "time-to-performance."

By the way, these results are better than just hypothetical. They're based on the actual results of a real-world company who applied the Workforce Optimization recipe!

Where To Go For Help

So where do Human Resources professionals turn to help optimize their company's employees? The majority of the time we rely on limited information to use to draw conclusions on recruiting, training, and development. We can call them educated assumptions or informed guesses, but they're still based mostly on limited information. It's sort of like sitting down in front of a jigsaw puzzle, and you know there's a picture of the Eiffel Tower in there somewhere, but you're not quite sure where it is and how to begin putting it together. The only problem is that this employee job performance puzzle has an almost infinite number of facets and nuances that make it even harder to sort out!

However, if you apply the principles in this book, most of which you are probably already doing as individual, somewhat disconnected, isolated, single-focused HR practices, but instead attack them as a whole, which is the heart of Workforce

Optimization, and you use the software tool I've included to help you organize and manage the power of the data, which will create for you true information, then the insight you'll have and the decisions that will come from it will help you deliver on the potential that is inherent in harnessing the collective power of your company's workforce. This book will take you, one piece at a time, through understanding the individual puzzle pieces, and the complex ways they fit together. It will walk you through putting your puzzle together.

Ready? Good! We'll start by assembling the border first, so first find all of the pieces with the flat sides to them. . .

Consider this: you need to decide where best for your company to invest its HR funds. At a minimum, you have to determine:

- What is the profile of the best candidates to hire?
- Where do we find the best candidates?
- How do we set proper expectations for newly hired people?
- Once we have the best candidates, what is the optimum path for them?
- What training courses produce the best results?
- What work or life experiences enhance job performance?
- What Managers produce the best results in the top performers?
- What tasks, at what level of performance, create the highest overall job results?
- Blah, blah, blah, etc., etc., etc. I think you can see where I'm going.

Where do you go for these answers? Suppose you could tap the performance indicators the company is already using in order to identify the top performers in the particular job in question? In the P.E.R.F.O.R.M. screen capture that follows, you'll see the "Peer Comparison Worksheet" form where I've selected the performance of a group of Sales people from a hypothetical branch in Detroit, chosen to review both their total sales figures and number of sales calls, picked a date range for a specific month, and sorted the list by who had the highest results for that month.

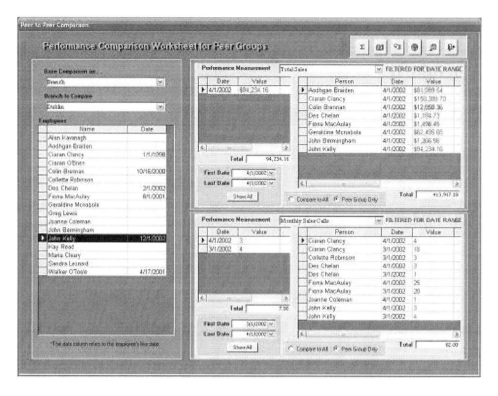

P.E.R.F.O.R.M. Screen– Performance Comparison Worksheet for Peer Groups

But now, what if I could trace the history of the top performers all the way back to the background they had when they first came to the company? The common threads would be the keys to the tough questions the company is looking to answer! The next P.E.R.F.O.R.M. screen capture shows an example of the rich history of information I get when I double click on a person's name in the Peer Comparison Worksheet, in this case, John Kelly.

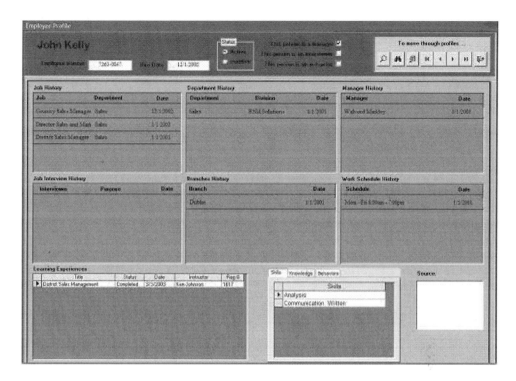

P.E.R.F.O.R.M. Screen– Employee Profile

Of course even more detail is available if I click or double-click on an entry in this screen, but this book is supposed to be more about the theory and techniques of Workforce Optimization, so I'll stop showcasing the software now. You'll see more about it as we move through the book anyway . . .

Ok, one more snapshot from P.E.R.F.O.R.M. . . . .

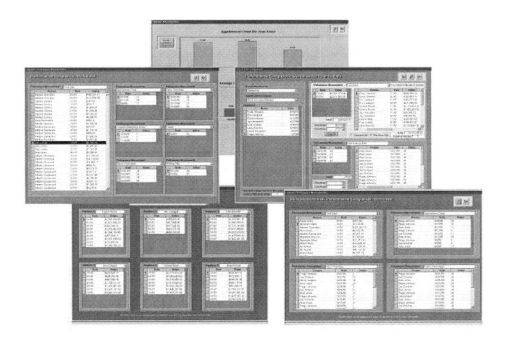

There are multiple Employee Performance Analysis forms that let you look at the data from many perspectives.

Using the **data to drive our decisions**, and basing HR Management investment in only those areas that have the most payoff, **supported by objective data** not subjective best guesses, is what Workforce Optimization is all about. There is tremendous power when we organize data into information! Using that insight is what enables us to design better training and development, identify more accurately the profile of top performers, and apply the art of using the science of Workforce Optimization to help a company realize higher results through better, more efficient, employee engagement.

While this book is meant to be a cohesive recipe for success, in much the same way that a recipe will only tell you to "add butter" but doesn't tell you all of the background of the history of butter making nor the pasteurization process, etc., etc., etc., this book will only give you the key attributes necessary for each ingredient. Mostly what this will be is a lengthy explanation of how the recipe works, not each ingredient. If the butter has to be melted, I'll tell you about melted butter and how to melt it. If the butter has to be chilled, we'll talk about chilled butter. To be certain, the outcome of your time in the kitchen will vary greatly if you use melted butter when you should have used chilled butter! Rest assured, if there are key attributes necessary in the individual components that contribute to a healthy Workforce Optimization environment, we'll spend the time to discuss those attributes. There is so much worthy material already in the public domain for several of these components that it would be overly redundant to detail them here. You will see references from time to time for those works which deal particularly well with one ingredient or another.

Ok, let's roll up our sleeves and get into the kitchen!!

The Key Ingredients

While we will look at almost all of the ingredients in a healthy Workforce Optimization environment, I'll apply one of the principles of good training design and introduce the essential elements first, and thereby lay the foundation for understanding the rest.

The real power of Workforce Optimization is to enable the business to, **at the same time**, manage both **individual things** (not just the "people" factor, but literally individual people, and not just the "jobs" factor but literally an individual job) and **things in aggregate**. It's sort of like using the age-old analogy of the forest and the trees. The subtle adjustment I'll make in order to fully use the analogy is that we'll manage the forest in total, but then we'll manage the collection of oak trees (perhaps the people element) separate from, but keeping in mind, the maple trees (perhaps the elements of the jobs), and both of those separate from, but keeping in mind, the forest grasslands (perhaps the company goals), etc. So far this analogy helps to explain two of the basic "forest management" areas, but there is also the third: the management of the individual oak tree (perhaps Bob or Sandy), while someone else is tweaking and pruning an individual shrub (perhaps the widget product the company makes.) Traditionally everyone has known that the components affect one another, I'm not staking any claim to being the first to discover that, but also traditionally efforts to literally cross-tie the elements and collectively manage them has stopped far short of the aspirations espoused in this recipe book, and have, in reality, been little more than cross-communication, along with a bit of cross-referencing. We're aspiring to the harder so we can reach higher ground!!

Perhaps another example of what achieving a Workforce Optimization environment looks like will help. A healthy W.O. environment is something like creating a winning sports team. If we were to define what a healthy, successful "team" is, I would vote for defining it as a **group of people where everyone knows both their own part to play**, and **the part that others play**, and, most importantly, **what each person, including themselves, is going to do in certain situations**. Using a baseball team as an example lends itself nicely to this discussion. When a certain batter on the opposing team comes up to bat, each player on the defending team makes small adjustments to where he/she is standing in anticipation of what that batter will most likely do. They know what pitch will be thrown, how that will most likely result in what sort of hit, and what they need to do in response. When the situation of opponents being on different bases changes, they know where to react first, second, and so on. As well, each person knows what he/she is to do when each other person on their team does what he/she will do if the ball goes to them. The pitcher knows that if the ball is hit to the outfield, he/she is to move into position to back up the second base player, in case the throw to second base is off. The catcher knows to move into position to back up the first base player, unless there is someone from the other team on second or third base, then he/she is to stay covering home plate. Etc., etc., etc. Now that's teamwork!!

My goal is not to explain the fundamentals of baseball, which is a good thing since I don't have much insight in that field (yes, that was an attempt at a play on words . . .) but rather to illustrate how winning teams work. Now someone once said that "great pitching wins baseball games." That may be true, but I'd love to see someone win a baseball game with great pitching and lousy catching! The quality of pitching is of greater importance because it comes to bear on every play in the game, but the reality is that **ALL OF THE PIECES, working together,** are necessary, and the degree to which one piece is weak, the entire team is weak. It's the reality that a chain is only as strong as its weakest link.

Now that we're all in tune with the baseball team analogy, let's apply it to the business world. When we talk about Workforce Optimization, the underlying strategy is to help each person in the workforce to realize his/her own potential IN A SPECIFIC ROLE, and to also get all of the individual workers to understand how his/her role fits into the larger workforce, and what the other workers are doing in specific situations, and thusly optimize the collective efforts of the workforce as a unit. Not every person can even perform a specific job or job task, and there are certainly those who will perform at a greater level than others in a specific job or job task. We've all heard the phrase "I was born to do this!" Well, reality is, that's true. Everyone has the ability to excel at something due to either his/her ability or attitude, or both, and step one in Workforce Optimization is to help each player find the right role, and then to get them doing their part as it fits into the great whole of the workforce collectively. Keep in mind, the player and the team are only 2/3 of the baseball analogy, there's a third aspect. Abner Doubleday, and probably several others, already did the work of defining the game of baseball itself. You most likely won't have that luxury. You're part of a dynamic organization that needs to constantly reinvent itself in order to stay competitive. In your world, not only does your baseball team need to be in a state of flux, but the game itself is constantly changing too!

The Recipe For The Main Course

That leads us to the point of being able to start defining the cross-wiring of the core elements of a healthy Workforce Optimization environment. If we're going to help optimize the players in the game, then we must be aware of and manage the inter-relation of the specific elements at work in each of the areas that comprise business and employee development. Managing the forest at the same time as we manage individual tress and groups of trees, as they all inter-relate, is the heart of Workforce Optimization and success in developing the potential of individuals and the workforce collectively.

There are no less than six core business elements, our list of key ingredients in our Workforce Optimization recipe, which must be related in the manner outlined in the table below. I hope you'll notice that these are the **generic categories**, and it's the details in each that are cross-wired, so that the categories are then properly cross-wired. There are more details in each area than what you'll find in this table, and we'll explore them in depth in later chapters, this table is meant to illustrate what I mean by managing the inter-relation, and to give us a foundation upon which to build. By the way, these are the real elements, not just made up ones for the purpose of having an illustration.

PLEASE DO NOT BE FOOLED!!! There are many more interdependencies in a Workforce Optimized company than those in this grid. These only represent the critical, absolutely-**must**-have components, which is meant to serve both to illustrate what I mean by the phrase "cross-wiring the elements" and also as a potential plan for a starting point if you are going to implement Workforce Optimization.

The first column tries to identify the essential elements of the key ingredient which need to be attended to if that category can be considered "complete and able to be cross-wired" with one or more of the other categories. The other columns represent how the elements of that category (you'll need to refer to column one for it to make sense, I think) are related to the elements of the six categories and 15 elements detailed in the intersecting row. Each relationship dependency is shown for the column and also for the row, so you can see them from the perspective of both categories. That explanation was probably more confusing than if I'd just let you take in the grid on your own. Sorry . . .

	The Company	Jobs	Employees	Customers	Products	HR & Training
The Company 1. Vision 2. Growth goals 3. Compensation planning 4. Department alignment	-	TC4<>J1<> HT1	TC2 <> E1 TC3 <> E3	TC2 <> C1		TC2 <> HT1 TC4<>J1<> HT1
Jobs 1. Job definition (processes and tasks) 2. Job outcomes & productivity standards	TC4<>J1<> HT1	-	J1 <> E2	J2 <> C2	J2 <> P1	J1 <> HT1 J1 <> HT2 J2 <> HT2 J2 <> HT3 J2 <> HT1 HT1 <> J1 TC4<>J1<> HT1
Employees 1. Community research 2. Personality mix 3. Tenure mix	TC2 <> E1 TC3 <> E3	J1 <> E2	-	E3<>C2<> P1	E3<>C2<> P1	E1 <> HT1 E1 <> HT3
Customers 1. Demographics 2. Needs & wants	TC2 <> C1	J2 <> C2	E3<>C2<> P1	-	E3<>C2<> P1	
Products 1. Type & volume, & price		J2 <> P1	E3<>C2<> P1	E3<>C2<> P1	-	-
HR &Training 1. Staffing 2. Job development planning 3. Individual development planning	TC2<>HT1 TC4<>J1<> HT1	J1 <> HT1 J1 <> HT2 J2 <> HT2 TC4<>J1<> HT1	E1 <> HT1 E1 <> HT3			-

A brief explanation of the hieroglyphics depicting the relationship elements might prove helpful, but keep in mind that lengthy explanations of all of these inter-dependencies, and more, are the contents of the following chapters:

TC2 <> E1	There must be a competitive alignment with the geographic area or quality employees will be hard to secure.
TC2 <> C1	There must realistically exist enough potential customers to validate growth goals.
TC2 <> HT1	There must be enough capable employees to support growth goals.
TC3 <> E3	Tenured employees are the result of many things, but compensation is certainly one of them.
TC4<>J1<>HT1	If the company is to realize it's vision, it will need people to focus on key areas, and this is best achieved by division of responsibility into company departments (TC4). However, when not hindered by geographic constraints, the departments should avoid job task redundancy. This may sound obvious, but 2 out of the 4 companies I worked for (50%!!) duplicated IT support in multiple departments. The skill level needed for distributed IT services was not supportable in the market from an HR staffing point of view nor cost effective from an ROI point of view, and, after much lost opportunity, they went back to centralized IT services. (They had originally changed from centralized IT to distributed IT because of perceived non-responsiveness.)
J1 <> E2	The tasks required by the job processes need to be of a type that can realistically be performed, and should be ones for which there are people who naturally enjoy doing them.
J2 <> C2	The output expectations (quality) from the jobs needs to be aligned with customer needs & wants.
J2 <> P1	The output expectations (quantity) from the jobs needs to be aligned with product volume demands.

J1 <> HT1	Once the job tasks are broken down into their enabling skills, knowledge, & behaviors, recruiting should find candidates closest to a match with top performers. A HALLMARK OF WORKFORCE OPTIMIZATION is to be able to identify, from past performance of top performers, what key backgrounds lead to best job performance.
J1 <> HT2	The job tasks should be directly tied to the learning outcomes of training & development activities. These are NOT the enabling skill, knowledge, or behavior elements, which may be reusable modules of a course. This refers to the goals of a course or other learning activity as being to enable someone to "DO" something, and that something should be a job task.
J2 <> HT2	The job expectations must have predetermined training materials which enables employees to master the job task to the level of acceptable performance.
J2 <> HT3	When job output expectations are not met, there must be healthy discussions with the employee to address the deficiencies.
J2 <> HT1	When job output expectations are not met after the healthy discussions, the employee must be released.
E1 <> HT1	From researching the community (E1) you'll will know what potential pools are available for recruiting (HT1.)
E1 <> HT3	You may have to expend more effort in development plans (HT3) if your local hiring pools have limited necessary skills, knowledge, or behavior.
E3<>C2<>P1	A function of business management is to match customers to products, BUT there is also a direct tie between the company having satisfied customers and its having satisfied (hence tenured, E3) employees. People work better when the company is successful.
HT1 <> J1	As recruiting efforts uncover common talents in the marketplace, job design should try to adapt to those innate skills, knowledge, or behaviors. E.g., If there are a lot of skateboarders in the area, try to find a way to use skateboarding in one or more of your company's job tasks.

In the grid you'll see references to classic elements of business management: company vision & goals, customers, and products. I am not intending to explain how to run or optimize those elements, there are far more detailed theories and books on those elements than require me to feebly attempt to further add detail, but rather the grid, and the dealings with those subjects later, are attempting to show how the results of those efforts tie into the efforts of the other areas, and all of them create the cross-wiring I'll be detailing later. As well, if this were intended to be a book on business, I'd certainly have a flawed table without the inclusion of "Financial Practices," along with a few others. That the company is attending to these other areas will be assumed but not included, as their details have less to do with the pieces that support Workforce Management, and there's only so many pages that I might hope for you to read. I have to cut things off somewhere . . .

Chapter Two:

Surveying the Forrest

- Defining the Business World

- What Leaders Have To Manage

- Product-Function-Process-Task Structure

- Strategic – Tactical – Functional Structure

Defining the Business World

Before we dig too deeply into how to optimize the workforce to achieve maximum results, let's take a quick moment to discuss business in general. After all, if we're trying to optimize the workforce of the modern company, it would be a good idea to have a working agreement of what these companies are.

Business Principles

Let's start our business definition with the two basic components: businesses must provide something worthwhile to the marketplace, and they must make a profit. The two components are co-dependent, you must have something worthwhile to offer or else people will not seek you out, and you must be "profitable" or else you won't last long. Even "non-profit" organizations need to be run with a mind to profit. They can rely on some level of a continued influx of cash, but this is rare, so the question posed to all businesses is really of "how much" profit is the company in pursuit. Compounding these two concerns are the two primary drivers of business which are always at play: revenue and cost. It is the balance of the two that makes a business successful. In reality, revenue is the primary of the two, so let's refer to the balancing act as "**focus on revenue** (sales), and manage cost."

While there is a litany of factors that must be managed if one is to run a business, understanding them all is **not** the purpose of this book. This book is concerned with understanding the one common element that all businesses share: the job performance of its employees. If business can be reduced to its two basic elements, let's carry the concept further to begin to understand the two basic elements that form its foundation. The healthy workforce is achieved by balancing two factors: the people and the environment in which they work. These two factors are co-dependent. To that end, we are looking into understanding those causal business factors that most directly impact the employee and/or the environment in which he/she works. The goal is higher job performance, but the factors to study and manipulate are the people and their work environment.

First let's look into the work environment. The business and its leaders are the people who are tasked with creating the environment in which the employees need to perform. How they build that environment and the world they create will have a profound affect on how well, or poorly, the employees can and do perform. I like to think of companies as "**people** doing **things** that result in **stuff** for which **customers** are willing to pay money." How do like that definition? Well, it's pretty basic, but that's how I like to start: basic.

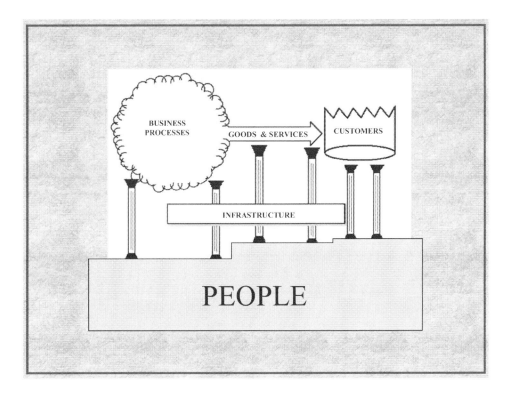

If you think about it, though, this is a basic model which all businesses follow. We can add definition and detail around each of the pieces of that definition, but the basic definition will give us the foundation on which to build. Think of it as the skeleton that holds together all of the muscles, blood vessels, and sinews that we'll be "fleshing" out (no pun intended, but I left it there all the same) throughout this book.

I've spent a lot of time looking at how to optimize the business processes that produce products, particularly with the Total Quality movement in America in the 80's and 90's, and still today, but this book primarily will focus on the one element that underlies all of the other: the **PEOPLE** of the company. It all comes down to your people. If we affect the factors that impact the people, then the people will be able to impact the company! I'll leave it to other writers who know much more than I to discuss how to get in touch with the voice of your customer, one of the elements in our basic business model, and still others to discuss how to manufacture goods and economic order quantity, and all the things that make up optimizing the production of goods and services, a second element of our basic business model. This recipe book is my attempt to pass on what I've learned from talking with others and from my own successes and failures, about how to help those who must make the basic business model work.

"It all comes down to your people!"

We're going to look extensively at optimizing the workforce, and this business model will give us a framework within which to understand what we're trying to optimize the workforce **to be able to do**. We are trying to optimize the workforce so that it will be able to set this basic business model into motion and keep it running to ever-increasing perfection. We want to help the workforce to be able to better understand the voice of the customer, or plan production, or create processes and procedures (that's part of what infrastructure is) and all the things needed to move the model. We won't get into the specifics of what needs to be done by these people for each of these elements, that's the job of the Workforce Optimization practitioners at each company, but the first step in optimizing the workforce for all of those specifics is to understand the strategies and techniques of Workforce Optimization in general.

Succinctly put: the goal of Workforce Optimization is to better enable the workforce to start and run the machine, represented by our basic business model.

Product – Function – Process – Task Breakdown

So let's take one more step further down the path of understanding what the generic machine is and how it is put together. Once upon a time, I had a job writing a procedures manual for the Information Services (IS) department of a large and successful company. I think I landed the job because of my Undergraduate degree in English, thinking "who better to WRITE a procedures manual than an English Major?" because it certainly wasn't because of my great IS background. I didn't have one at the time!

Maybe it was because I was giddy from writing operating procedures, maybe it was because it was the 80's and we were in the midst of adopting the Total Quality Management technique of "re-engineering business processes," whatever the source, I realized one day that if we want to tackle efficiencies, we need to bring structure to the chaos. Maybe I'm just a neat freak. After all, you can't re-engineer chaos, and you certainly can't train someone how to do it, and you can forget about writing a procedures manual explaining the steps of how to do it!

I found myself in desperate need of a way to think of the company and its components. If I was going to write an efficient procedures manual, I needed to consider not just the steps of a single task, but also the inter-relation to others in other areas and *how, when, and where* they picked up the output of the procedures on which my group was focused. In short, I needed to have a better, easier to understand and explain to others, way to look at the structure of "the machine," the basic business model, but with one more layer of definition and detail.

The result of my epiphany was that I developed a way to organize the business unit by thinking of the **Functions** that it conducted in support of the **Products** the company offered. The functional areas then get broken down into the **Processes** that result in the products, and the processes get defined by the **Tasks** (or steps) in the process. The whole structure is referred to as the Product-Function-Process-Task breakdown, or P-F-P-T for short.

You can apply the Product/Function level starting at a department within a company, and look at the internal "products" the department offers to the company. At the time I was part of the Information Services Department, so we applied the P-F-P-T breakdown to the department, and organized in terms of the "products" that the IS Department created within the company. In this situation, the "products" of the IS Department were: computer programs (we called them "applications"); change management; employee workstations; information distribution; and disaster recovery.

The Function level became the various groups within these "product" lines. I was part of the change management and information distribution groups. We handled system security, data integrity, and report generation and distribution. For each of these we had several processes that resulted in some element important to each function, and of course we had defined tasks (or steps) in each process. We mapped and remapped in an effort to drive every inefficient step out of every process, and to combine tasks whenever possible to serve multiple processes. It was a well-run machine!

Efficiency and predictability are the output of P-F-P-T. My guess is that your company's departments have some variation of this concept in place too. That would be a good thing, and something we'll use for even greater gains when we get to the interrelation of the elements in this ecosystem.

As we look at optimizing the workforce, it is much easier to identify those things that help by defining, dissecting, examining, and referring to them in the context of their place in the P-F-P-T structure. Don't worry if you don't have everything detailed in this way, you can still start by looking at the jobs and the tasks performed by people doing them. I'd suggest tackling the "larger world" structure, but don't let that hold you back from getting started in the "smaller world" structure: job tasks.

Once we had the P-F-P-T structure put into place, then we were able to use that definition to focus on how to optimize what we wanted people to do that resulted in these great products. The Workforce Optimization techniques kicked in, and the process tasks were further defined by the Skills, Knowledge, and Behaviors needed to perform them We'll talk at length about skills, knowledge, and behaviors (s,k,&b's) throughout the rest of the book, but I wanted to introduce the concept now to start showing the cross over from the business unit side of the house over to the HR side of the house. The business units use job tasks to analyze process efficiencies towards output, the HR concerns use job tasks as a road map to ability acquisition. The beauty of all of this is that both use the same common ground: job tasks! Effort by each is a benefit to other!

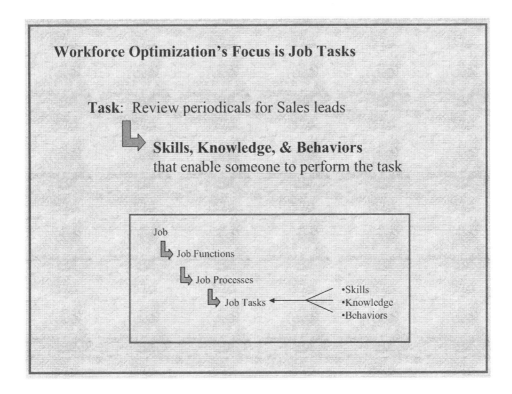

What Leaders and Managers Have To Focus On

As we look at the concept of Product-Function-Process-Task, please keep in mind that I'm NOT referring to the organizational structure of companies whereby they group into levels of who does what. Traditionally, companies have groups of people who focus on **strategic** issues, those who take the strategic vision and translate it into an executable **tactical** level, and then those who do the things of the company at a **functional** level. All three are necessary to make a company operate smoothly, and all three have their particular sets of skill and ability requirements.

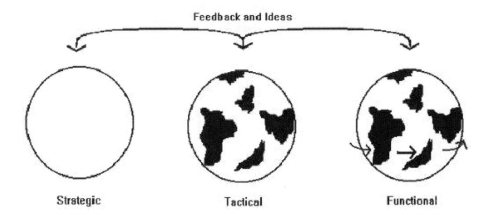

Feedback and Ideas

Strategic   Tactical   Functional

I don't want to turn this into a recipe book for How To Manage or even How To Lead, but this is one element of the recipe for Workforce Optimization. Later in this book we'll get to what needs to be done by someone in the role of a manager, but here I'd like to talk a minute with you about a slightly different idea than the different types of managers. We are talking about business in general, but you're going to have to avoid the temptation of translating this "Strategic, Tactical, and Functional" concept into "Upper Management, Middle Management, and Front-line Employees," because that is **NOT** what I'm trying to portray.

What this use of "Strategic, Tactical, and Functional" is about is an attempt to give us a common way to think about how business is conceived. It must first go through a visionary phase, and this is accomplished by those who see the "big picture" of the company and its value in the marketplace. They "define and shape" the company and create strategies for how to get from where the company is to where the vision wants to take it. That's why these things are considered the "strategic" level, because out of them comes the company's vision and strategies to achieve the vision.

From there, another phase starts where someone takes the vision and the strategies and translates that into tactical things that can and need to be done to achieve the vision. This is where day-to-day tasks are conceived and defined, keeping in mind particularly the inter-relation of ideas, events, and tasks. The

Tactical level takes the world that was created in the Strategic level and gives it definition.

Then the Functional level takes over and makes the world turn! The degree to which the Strategic and Tactical levels have done a good job, including obtaining a real-world perspective and then effective hand-off, will determine if and how well the Functional level is able to perform the things developed and defined on a day in and day out basis. The question is: "does the machine 'function' when it's time to produce?" so hence the name for this level: the Functional level.

All of this calls for great levels of interaction and communication, both Strategic to Tactical to Functional, and Functional to Tactical to Strategic. Most often there will be those who for whatever reason, sometimes giftedness and sometimes just being in the right place at the right time, are exclusively members of one of these levels. The way the Strategic-Tactical-Functional structure works at a functional level is that members from the Strategic level will deal with the tasks of the Strategic level, and then interact with members of the Tactical level to further define and create, and then eventually hand-off the output of the Strategic level for them to take over and do their Tactical level stuff to. The Tactical level members then spend time amongst themselves doing their tactical level stuff, and then interact with those members of the Functional level to further define and create, and then eventually hand-off the output of the Tactical level to the Functional level.

A healthy company needs all three levels doing their thing in order to exist and grow. I'm not naive enough to think that all of these people should get paid the same, but I am wise enough to think that all of these people should be treated the same: fairly. While we'll talk more about "fair" as we progress, I'll take a moment here to remind all of us of the sayings "the worker is worth his wages," and "don't muzzle the ox while he is treading out the grain." Both are good mottos to apply if you want the highest attitudes from the members of the workplace "family."

The reason I wanted to take this whole "strategic-tactical-functional digression is so that we can talk about the workings of our simple business model ("the machine") using several different points of reference. Sometimes we'll talk about enabling the workforce to perform its tasks from a P-F-P-T breakdown point of view, but sometimes we will want to look at those things that are done from a Strategic-Tactical-Functional point of view. For example, there are things that one must do as a practitioner of Workforce Optimization that are of a <u>strategic</u> nature. These things define Workforce Optimization in its vision, goals, and strategies. Once that is in place, we'll turn our attention to the <u>tactics</u> of how to achieve the vision. Lastly, we'll look at who needs to do what from a task-oriented <u>functional</u> perspective. You might say that the Function of Workforce Optimization (in the P-F-P-T perspective) has its requirements at all three of the Strategic, Tactical, and Functional levels.

As a good Workforce Optimization practitioner, you'll need to keep in mind that you'll need to examine and understand your "machine" from at least these two basic points of view: P-F-P-T and S-T-F. Try saying those three times, fast.

Where Do We Start The Job/Employee Match Up?

I'm going to recommend that the very first step in planning our fine dining experience for the company is to start with the business units, after all, that's who we're trying to support. Step one in the implementation of Workforce Optimization is to understand the business units and the functions, processes, and tasks that they are performing. Often this is best accomplished by looking at the jobs present in the organization.

Fair warning, don't be blinded by what you find. There's a 50/50 chance that the organization has poor job structure simply as a result of the evolutionary nature to how companies grow. I'm not going to elaborate on Organizational Development theory and techniques here, that would take up a library in and of itself. For this topic, I'll refer you to an excellent book by Louis Carter, W. Warner Burke, Edward E. Lawler III, Beverly L. Kaye, Jay Alden Conger, John Sullivan, David Giber (Editor), and Marshall Goldsmith (Editor), forward by Richard F.

Beckhard, entitled Best Practices in Organization Development and Change: Culture, Leadership, Retention, Performance, Coaching. With all those people contributing, it HAS to be good! (and it is!)

For our discussion in this book, realize that this is one of the pieces to spend time looking at. You may not have any influence on how the company sets up its jobs, or it may be within your complete control, either way, once you have the organization's jobs structured adequately, then you'll need to list them out in order to satisfy step one in our Workforce Optimization implementation.

Chapter Three:
What Is This New Buzz Word
"Workforce Optimization"?

- Defining "Workforce Optimization"

- Measuring Business Results

- Measuring Employee Job Performance

Defining "Workforce Optimization"?

Now that we have a foundational working definition of what companies are, let's start to talk about how Human Resources professionals can help the company better work with employees in an effort to boost the results. Let's talk about *Workforce Optimization!*

Great! Just what we need, another HR buzzword! I can hear the moaning from here. I'd probably moan too if I weren't trying to popularize the concept and therefore needed some sort of label for it. Sorry! Hey, if you can come up with a better label I'm all for it. For now we'll have to get along with "Workforce Optimization" because it's the best I can come up with. So let me try to explain it, and maybe you'll be a little more inclined to use it yourself.

Put simply, Workforce Optimization is managing the elements that contribute to or inhibit greater job performance, either individually or collectively. Trying to paraphrase the concept as succinctly as possible, Workforce Optimization refers to the attempt to use **IN AGGREGATE**, several of the elements of traditional HR Management, in concert with several traditional elements of business unit management, to create an environment whereby the efforts of the workforce are optimized. If we are going to the trouble to recruit good people, we typically are already smart enough to know that we should understand what the job entails and the makeup of a successful performer, and then look for people who best match that profile. We may even be smart enough to know what learning activities best enhance performance for someone in the job, but are we smart enough to know that we should understand what learning activities, in connection with what background, in connection with what manager checking and coaching, results in top performance. And if we're smart enough to know that we should understand this complex interrelation, do we have an efficient way to put our finger on those pulse points?

What better career could you possibly choose than to be involved in helping employees realize their maximum potential?! When managed as a profit center, the HR function not only helps people, but it also gives a company a strategic, competitive advantage. When people are more fully engaged as employees, they work smarter, more creatively, and with passion. These behaviors are the building blocks of world-class employees, which create and sustain world-class organizations. When the workforce is more highly fitted to perform its job tasks, then it produces higher results with fewer resources. That's business efficiency, and **it all comes down to your people.** Work with optimizing the people, and you, by cause and effect, optimize the results the people achieve. That's a competitive advantage that you can count on!

While you may acquire some new insights as you read this book, what will most likely turn out to be the best gain for having purchased it at such a great bargain price is the software program that accompanies it. As I've practiced the art of applying the science of HR management for almost 20 years, I've been hampered by the lack of a decent tool to help me as I've tried to understand and manage these interrelations. There simply was no easy-to-use tool, so I was left to shuffle and sort through a mountain of binders and system reports. I'll be pontificating as politely as I can about how I understand the puzzle pieces of employee job performance fit together, but I am also sharing the software program that I created to help me practically apply these techniques. Without a useable tool, I think we're going to be treading water for a long time.

Now, back to the topic at hand: understanding the business world. As our complex diagram from the last chapter (that was meant to be a joke, it's not complex at all . . .) shows, the foundation of all business structures is the people the company is relying on to perform all of the things that must happen to produce the "stuff" that customers are willing to pay for. Enter the Human Resources Management specialists! To help achieve maximum results through the workforce, companies turn to HR professionals to assist the organization in better use of the elements that center on the people. Too often then, in an effort to prove value, the HR Dept. takes too heavy of a hand in dictating who to hire, when to review them, and how to fire them. The result is resentment and complete breakdown of the partnership. I won't belabor this point, let's just leave the subject with the warning that unless your HR group is working with the vision/mission of "supporting the business units" then we should stop here and adjust that attitude or else Workforce Optimization will never become a reality in your company.

Now, back to the topic at hand - understanding the business world. Again. The goal of any HR Management approach should be to support the business unit in their need for the top performers in all jobs at all levels. This, however, is easier said than achieved. I believe the core reason for the difficulty is that it is nearly impossible to manage all of the components behind such a goal, and it only becomes even remotely possible with a good tool to help in the effort, as I mentioned before. Before, then, we start to look at how to manage the three-ring circus, or to keep with my cookbook analogy, to serve the full-course meal, let's start our list of what those individual components are. I reserve the right to add to the list as we go along. I don't want to overwhelm you with all of them at once. At a minimum, a good HR Management approach will consider:

- jobs present in the company;
- reward/punishment triggers for each job;
- career paths available from job to job;
- skills, knowledge, and behaviors needed for each job;
- employee growth and accountability reviews (they're two separate things!)
- recruitment sources;
- interview and hiring processes;
- development programs for job performance improvement;
- training results (class, job, and company impact);

Ok, I'm tired of the list, so my guess is you're REALLY tired of the list. Let's throw this around by looking at a picture, in an effort to save us both a thousand words.

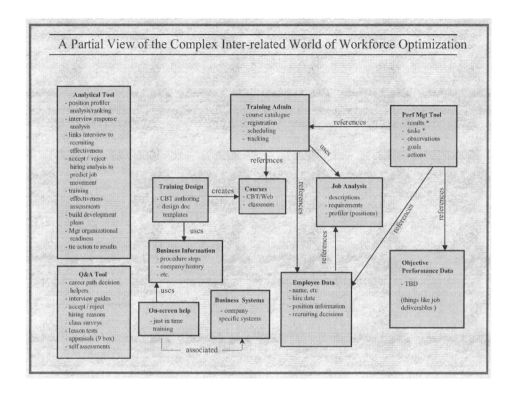

A Partial View of the Complex Inter-related World of Workforce Optimization

As I already warned you, this is only the starting point. There are many more factors that affect the job performance of people. We haven't even scratched the surface of things like work environment and changes to it, compensation plans (not just more money), company competitiveness trends and how HR Management adjustments are made for different situations. The key point of this section is to realize that we must address the individual items, but the real success comes in how we manage the **interrelation** of the components. We must design with the big picture in mind, understand the end we are after, and then build or adjust the individual pieces so they better fit the larger puzzle. Sometimes that means we will make sacrifices in how we manage the individual pieces if the larger gain is worth the smaller loss. For example, I may choose to release a person from a training event at 80% job performance in order to have them available for some other use instead of holding them back until they are at 90% or higher. The smaller focus of an additional 10% mastery level may cause a negative effect in some larger focus, keeping the larger focus from achieving its result.

To help understand the pieces of the puzzle that must be looked at and managed in aggregate if we are to optimize our workforce, I think it is easier to think of them in groups. In short, Workforce Optimization considers these things:

- ✓ things having to do with the company in general (it's goals, success measurements, jobs, and employee expectations);
- ✓ things having to do with how the company develops its employees' abilities (training classes, registration for those classes, and career plans);

    things having to do with employees (their demographic info, work history at the company, and prior work life and work experience);

    and lastly, and most importantly, things having to do with how well each employee performs his/her job tasks.

It's a lot to manage, but you'll soon see it is possible, and it is worth the effort!

Here our first Workforce Optimization Maxim presents itself, and, interestingly enough, it's one of the same ones present in business in general.

Think of it as everything we do in the HR Management world must support the goal of the company. What is the primary goal of any company? To be profitable. Therefore, everything we do in the HR Management world must be directly traceable to the profitability of the company. There's no room in any company for self-serving tasks. If someone is doing something that doesn't lead to business results, then it's wasteful and must be driven from the company. And sometimes that means the people who created and/or perpetuated it must be driven out too!

> **Workforce Optimization Maxim #1: The purpose of Workforce Optimization is to maximize business results.**

Let's see, how about an example? Hmm. Ok, what happens to those annual employee reviews? Hmmm. You know most companies I talk with tell me their annual reviews go into a file and are never heard from again, and that would be a good thing. Why a good thing? Well, that would mean that the employee it's for isn't suing the company, because that's the only time an annual review is used, after the initial use of it as a means of setting up the compensation discussion. We'll talk more about those later. For now, let's close this discussion with an agreement that the annual review should at least become the coaching plan for the year. Now I know you'll tell me that's what they're use is now, but that's probably where the lack of a good tool comes in. Forms on paper, or even forms in MSWord aren't going to be much good. My suggestion: use P.E.R.F.O.R.M. We'll talk about how P.E.R.F.O.R.M. supports the review process when we get to that later.

Workforce Optimization's Goal

There should be a clear path tying back to the money!

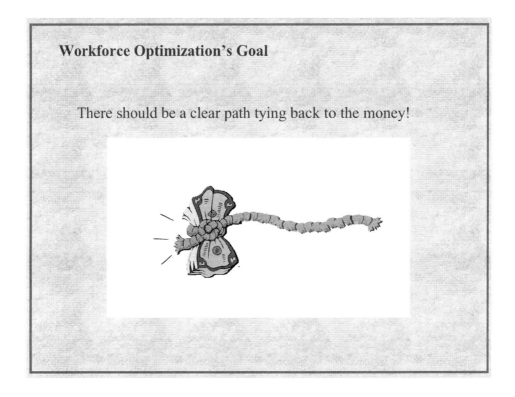

Workforce Optimization shifts the paradigm of seeing the contribution of the HR group away from that of a "necessary evil" to more of a "competitive advantage." When the HR Management approach delivers on the goal of getting top performers in place faster and at an ever increasing performance level, we become a powerful competitive edge, not just the people that keep the company from getting sued by unhappy employees, or ex-employees.

We're just going to chip away at the tip of the P.E.R.F.O.R.M. iceberg for now, because there are several areas of P.E.R.F.O.R.M. that come together to support Workforce Optimization. As we tackle each area of Workforce Optimization from the business side of things, we'll pop over to the systems part of the house and talk about how P.E.R.F.O.R.M. supports that element. For now, we're ready to look at how P.E.R.F.O.R.M. supports looking at business results as the key determinant of success of the Human Resources function.

As you build your data a little at a time, over time, P.E.R.F.O.R.M. will consolidate it into relational forms that will let you manage this crossover chain. The first place where we start to collect company information is the Business Results area. You can better understand how, if we want to truly understand and manage an employee's job performance, we need to easily see the tie back to the profit drivers of the company. P.E.R.F.O.R.M. lets you catalog this sometimes hard to follow chain of linked business elements. In a sense, P.E.R.F.O.R.M. helps the company understand its own complicated inter-relations by organizing them into related forms that can be moved through with a click of a button. From the Business Results form, I can see (and drill down to) all of the measurements the company uses to gauge, and keep a finger on the pulse of, results. The Business Results form also lets us quickly see (and drill down to) the jobs in the company where things are done that ultimately lead to achieving each business result. Once again, a critical path that is sometimes hard to find, let alone follow.

The tie between business results, performance measurements, jobs, and job tasks is more fully described in the previous section of this recipe book entitled *What Is This New Buzz Word "Workforce Optimization?"* and the subsequent one entitled *"Building Business Unit Bridges."*

Measuring Business Results

As we started to understand companies earlier, the starting point is to look at what the company is trying to achieve. We called them "business

Required Learning | Interview Questions | Career Path | Job Success Enablers | Skills | Knowledge | Behaviors | Job Accountability Factors | Job Task Performance Measurements

results," and so you'll find a corresponding area of P.E.R.F.O.R.M. that let's you catalog the company's desired Business Results. When you click on that button in the Company Info area of the Main Menu, you'll see the Business Results form open.

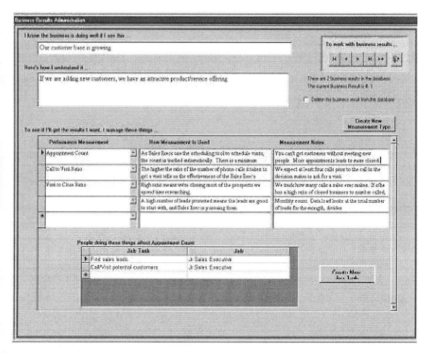

P.E.R.F.O.R.M. Screen– Business Results Administration

Here is an explanation of the fields and buttons on this form:

Item Name	What It's For
I know the business is doing well if I see this . . .	This is the business result itself. Typically stated in terms of a company goal.
Here's how I understand it	More importantly, how the company thinks this is a gauge of success.

Required Learning | Interview Questions | Career Path | Job Success Enablers | Skills | Knowledge | Behaviors | Job Accountability Factors | Job Task Performance Measurements

Delete	Check box to use if you no longer want this entry. on a regular basis, the P.E.R.F.O.R.M. Systems Analyst will purge all items flagged by a user for deletion.
Create New Measurement Type Button	Use this to open the Performance Measurement form if you do not see a choice you want to link to this Business Result and need to create a new one.

There can be as many Business Results records as the company deems it possible to manage. These can be a catalog of just high-level company goals, or they can also include Department goals. This is the place to look if someone wants to understand what the company is trying to achieve.

What makes this form so useful is that each Business Result is tied to the measurements that the company will use to gauge how well or poorly they are doing in pursuit of that result. I had a wise boss who used to say "Don't expect what you don't inspect." It's an adage that proves it's worth time and again. No wise company creates a goal and then has no way to measure it's progress against that goal. By tying the desired Business Result to its corresponding Performance Measurement, we know what measurements are the ones to focus on if we want to achieve results. The idea behind associating a Performance Measurement to a Business Result is that, if one wants to achieve the result, which you can't manage against because it's too big and too nebulous, one can focus on doing something to affect the underlying performance that is tracked by the Performance Measurement, and, thusly, do things that can be managed, that ultimately, lead to the Business Results the company values.

Measuring Employee Job Performance

So, behind the Business Results form are the Performance Measurements that let someone attack the larger goal in bite-sized pieces. In order to have these available for selection and linking, there is a section of

Required Learning | Interview Questions | Career Path | Job Success Enablers | Job Accountability Factors | Skills | Knowledge | Behaviors | Job Task Performance Measurements

One Performance Measurement can be an indicator for more than one Business Result. We create the "catalog" of all of the Performance Measurements used by the company here, in the Performance Measurement form, and then they are available for selecting in other places.

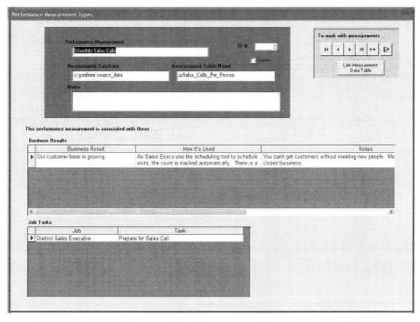

P.E.R.F.O.R.M. Screen– Performance Measurements Types

To make it easy to remember how these Performance Measurements cross-relate to the Business Results, you'll see displayed on the Performance Measurement form the Business Results to which it has been related over on the Business Results form. The same holds true for the display at the bottom of the form. We haven't looked at it yet, but there is another area of P.E.R.F.O.R.M. that lets you catalog the jobs and the job tasks (we'll get to those very soon, I assure you) people do at this company. As we look at someone performing a job task, there is a trail of relationship back to these Performance Measurements.

Here is an explanation of the fields, buttons, and tabs on this form:

Item Name	What It's For
Performance Measurement	This is the name by which the company can recognize this measurement. This is the name that will appear in any drop-down lists.
ID #	Ref. Number assigned and used by P.E.R.F.O.R.M..
Delete	Check box to use if you no longer want this entry. On a regular basis, the P.E.R.F.O.R.M. Systems Analyst will purge all items flagged by a user for deletion.
Measurement Database	References the physical database in which this data is stored. This field is usually completed by a P.E.R.F.O.R.M. System Analyst.
Measurement Table Name	References the actual name of the table that has this data. This field is usually completed by a P.E.R.F.O.R.M. System Analyst.
Notes	To help anyone who is wondering what this measurement is or how it's used.

A Quick Note on P.E.R.F.O.R.M. Navigation

Throughout P.E.R.F.O.R.M. you're going to see the same buttons appear over and over. I thought I'd take a moment here to explain their use. As is true for many items in P.E.R.F.O.R.M., if you park your mouse pointer over in item and let it sit for a second, a tip will appear to try to help explain what that item is for. This applies to buttons and fields, so try the tips whenever you're not sure why something is on a form.

Required Learning | Interview Questions | Career Path | Job Success Enablers | Skills | Knowledge | Behaviors | Job Accountability Factors | Job Task Performance Measurements

Here is an explanation of the rest of the form:

Item Name	What It's For
	Closes whatever form you are in.
	Let's you move from one record to another. The far left button takes you to the very first record, while the far right one lets you create a brand new record. Use the Tip to find out what each button does if you're not sure, but I think you'll be able to figure these out.
	This is the "Search" button. It lets you look through a sorted list for the record you are after.
	Hmmm . . . I wonder? You got it – print a report. Some forms have multiple reports, so there are multiple buttons. Use the Tip to find out what report is printed by each button. I think you'll be able to figure these out too.
Record: 14 ◀ 1 ▶ ▶l ▶▶ of 1	These "record bars" show up in some forms and subforms. Not only do they let you know where you are in a list, they also let you move back and forth. If you want to jump to a specific place in the list, you can type a number in the area where the current record number is displayed and then press the Enter key.

Create New Measurement Type Form Specific Buttons	These buttons usually mean what they say. If you click them, that's what they'll do. These change from form to form, so, if you're not sure what they do, use the Tip feature.
	This button shows up in several places, and allows you to credit the employee with all the skills, knowledge, and behaviors associated with the item you are working in. For example, when working with a class registration, this button credits a participant with all the s,k,&b associated with all the tasks that are learning outcomes for the course.
	Just a quick plug for the Miscellaneous Factors area of P.E.R.F.O.R.M. This button shows up all over the place, and it opens a form that lets you see/record any off-the-wall factor, either that is specific to a person or to an entire group, that may turn out later to affect job performance. See the section on this for more details about how it works.
Double-Click	The forms are set up to help you easily move from one area to a related area, or to "drill down" to a deeper layer of detail by simply double-clicking your left mouse button.
Sub-menus	If you single-click your right mouse button you will access a sub-menu for the form or sub-form you are in.

Required Learning | Interview Questions | Career Path | Job Success Enablers | Job Accountability Factors | Job Task Performance Measurements | Skills | Knowledge | Behaviors

In the sub-menu - ↕ Sort Ascending ↕ Sort Descending	These are a powerhouse!! Anytime you are in a field on a form and you want to sort the data behind the form by that single field, click on that field to move the focus there, then access the submenu, then use the sort options to sort it the way it will help. If you are in a form or sub-form that is a list, you can highlight more than one column and then use the sort feature and P.E.R.F.O.R.M. will sort by first the leftmost column and then sub-sort by each column to the right.
Move a column	If you click on a column heading in a list, P.E.R.F.O.R.M. will select the entire column. You can then click and hold your left mouse button to "grab" the highlighted column (or columns) and drag it (them) to a new place. This is helpful if you want to do sort and sub-sorts on multiple columns.
Full Windows Features	P.E.R.F.O.R.M. is a Windows based application, so all of the features you're used to in Windows applications work here too. You can copy/paste data within P.E.R.F.O.R.M. or even out to another Windows program (e.g., MSExcel). You can select list data and create quick graphs and charts. My advice: if you've done it in another program, try it in P.E.R.F.O.R.M. Chances are it'll work. If it doesn't, write to us and we'll make it work! Editor@RSMSOL.com.

The left margin contains vertical tabs reading: Required Learning | Interview Questions | Career Path | Job Success Enablers | Skills | Knowledge | Job Accountability Factors | Behaviors | Job Task Performance Measurements

Chapter Four:

The Key Connections Between Business Units and Workforce Optimization

- Building Business Unit Bridges

- Job Processes and Tasks

- Job Tasks and Learning Outcomes

- Job Performance Measurement

- Measuring Learning Success

Building Business Unit Bridges

Of all the essential aspects of a Workforce Optimization environment, perhaps the most important of all is the integration of HR Management elements with the business unit infrastructure. What that means is that, whenever possible, the work done by the business units should be re-used to create the related elements of HR Management. Since, once again, a picture is worth a thousand words, here's a chart showing some of the elements that are created by the business side of the house and how they relate to items used to find and develop employees on the HR side of the house.

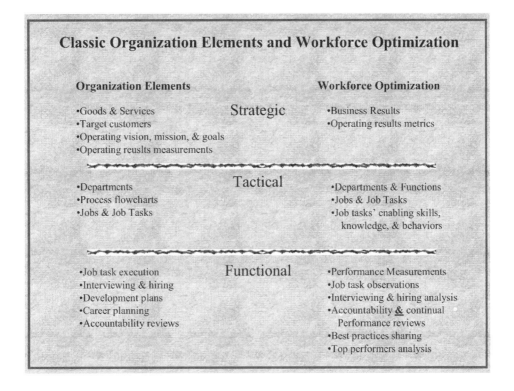

Classic Organization Elements and Workforce Optimization

Organization Elements		Workforce Optimization
	Strategic	
•Goods & Services		•Business Results
•Target customers		•Operating results metrics
•Operating vision, mission, & goals		
•Operating reuslts measurements		
	Tactical	
•Departments		•Departments & Functions
•Process flowcharts		•Jobs & Job Tasks
•Jobs & Job Tasks		•Job tasks' enabling skills, knowledge, & behaviors
	Functional	
•Job task execution		•Performance Measurements
•Interviewing & hiring		•Job task observations
•Development plans		•Interviewing & hiring analysis
•Career planning		•Accountability & continual Performance reviews
•Accountability reviews		•Best practices sharing
		•Top performers analysis

The cross-over between classic organization elements and Workforce Optimization is perhaps best understood by looking at one of the most overlooked, yet most valuable payoff common puzzle pieces: **job tasks**.

Job Processes and Tasks

In the wake of Total Quality Management, there are few companies that have not ardently codified the products they offer by diagramming and documenting the business processes that create them. By the time we reached the new century, virtually every process had been work-team analyzed, re-engineered, and statistically process measured into a state of ultimate perfection. I seriously applaud those efforts, especially since I was part of organizations that championed those initiatives. The results have been evidenced by the continuance of these approaches to optimize the work processes that companies employ.

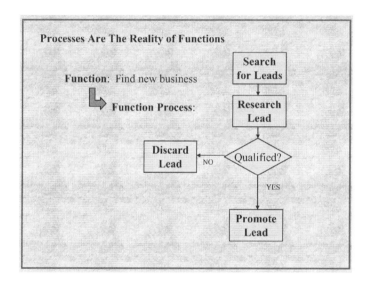

"What should HR Management techniques do with all that hard work and excellent detail of job potential?" Why the answer is simple: use it! When we start to look for the basis of training and development efforts, we need look no further than what the business unit has already taken the pains to define – the business processes. As we seek to help people succeed in their jobs, what we're really trying to help them do is to execute the tasks that need to be done as part of their job function. Job functions, in order to best optimize them, are naturally broken down by the processes they embody.

There is a wealth of opportunity available to the Workforce Optimization effort if we consider the fundamental component of process analysis: the **job tasks!**

Think of it as though the business unit is driving down to finer granularity along the path of customer deliverables, as we discussed in the P-F-P-T section a minute ago. Along the parallel path, the Human Resources Management groups are driving up a broadening path of employee enablement. The two paths share the common stepping-stone in the path that is **"job tasks."**

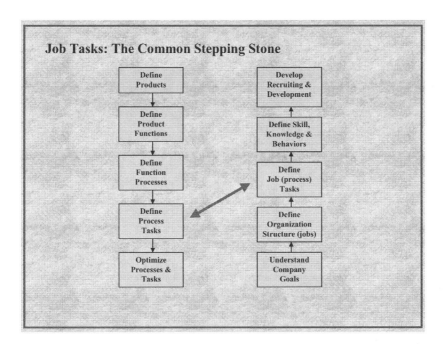

There has been a lot of attention paid in the past to job competencies. I recall when I was a fledgling IT Supervisor having a tremendous struggle making the connection between how I was to review the performance of the team I lead in terms of their mastery of their job competencies. I was too focused on how well or poorly they were executing the tasks of their job. Maybe I'm unique in my ignorance, but I think not. In fact I know not, because once I admitted my stumbling with the approach, several of my peers chimed in. I'll never forget how confusing it was to me as a member of the business unit to try to evaluate and coach someone against a job competency.

"So if job competencies are such a good idea (which, as a member of the HR community I hold to be true,) then how do we meet the business unit community on grounds with which they are more comfortable?"

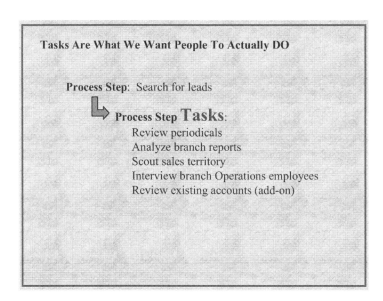

The answer is the **job tasks!** If you consider that most processes in the business unit are already defined by their job tasks, then it is a short step for the Workforce Optimization effort to adopt them for their purpose. When you consider that one of the primary goals of HR Management is to deliver to the business unit someone trained to the highest possible measure, the natural question is "trained to do what?" The answer, first is "his or her job." That begs the question "what does that mean?" And that brings us to the natural conclusion "the TASKS that he or she must correctly perform in order to participate in the job's processes."

The best way to design a training and development event is to consider how it will enable a person to perform one or more tasks required by one or more of the business processes of the company!

The tie between the business unit world and the HR Management world through the job tasks is a simple one with huge rewards. If you define jobs as to their tasks, and the skills, knowledge, and behaviors needed to do the tasks, you can:

Target recruiting and interviewing

Test candidates for foundation skills, knowledge, and/or behaviors

Develop learning activities that enhance ability to perform specific job tasks, using **modules** that develop s/k/b's

Accelerate learning time for new employees by teaching job <u>foundation</u> s/k/b's, then building higher-level ability.

If you define how job tasks tie back to the key success measurements which the organization has put in place, you can:

Target improvement to those things that have the highest yield

Base your development interventions on empirical data

Watch the measurements to see the resulting impact of your efforts

We're still left with defining the skills, knowledge, and behaviors requisite to perform a job task, and also the enabling learning components, but we are truly in partnership with the business unit as we offer learning activities to the employee, and, more importantly, as we work with the business unit to develop the learning activities that enhance the work performance of their employees. **There is no extra work to be done on the part of the business unit managers in order for effective training to be delivered!** We are simply reusing the results of their previous efforts to codify their business processes. As we tackle the chore of creating learning events that enhance job performance, we also already have a great starting point because the key components of what is to be trained towards is already in place – the job's tasks.

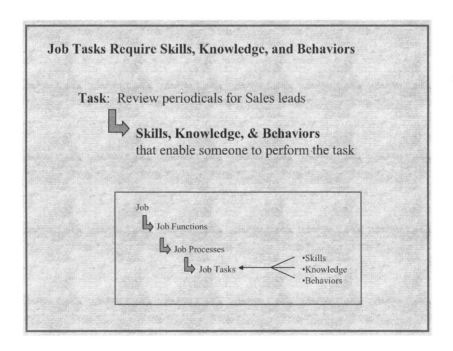

Think of it as someone "doing a job" has the "ability" to perform a task. That's what "doing their job" consists of: the ability to complete individual tasks. The ability to complete a task is actually the result, or compilation, of the smaller building blocks of skills, knowledge, and behaviors that build up into the "ability" to perform a job task. If I'm going to do the job task of driving nails, in the process of framing a structural wall, I need skills such as hand-eye coordination, hammer grasping, and nail holding, but I also need the knowledge of how deep to sink the nails, how hard to strike them so they penetrate the wood without bending, and how far apart to space them. But all of that is worthless if I don't have the behaviors of Attention to Detail and Pride of Workmanship so that I make sure I don't deviate from what I know I need to do.

As you identify these component building blocks, you begin to see where some skills, some knowledge, and some behaviors are needed for many job tasks, and often by different jobs. That will help you prioritize what training components to develop. Those that can be used by the most people are the ones to build first.

But it's not that easy . . .

Sometimes a component skill, knowledge, or behavior is only used by one job for one job task, but it is such a **critical element**, and enables such an **important task**, that is tied to something that results in really **important job impact**, that contributes to something **highly valued** by the company because it results in something **customers are willing to pay for** (do you see the importance of knowing this value chain?!) that, even though it's only used once, you will devote a lot of time, energy, and perhaps money to sorting out how to train it well.

Ok, I'll settle down now … I still recall, though, my growing excitement when this epiphany first struck me. I hope you can see the same widening view of the obstacles that are removed once we realize the power of reusing job tasks as the key building blocks to training design and development.

There is a connection between someone having certain behaviors and their ability to acquire certain skills, which, in turn enables them to excel at the tasks that require those skills. If you want to think of it as the behaviors are prerequisites for acquiring skills, I think that is a safe perspective.

The qualifier to that perspective is to distinguish the role which **innate behavior** differs from **acquired behavior**. For example, leadership is a combination of leadership behavior (you could call them "traits" if you want) and leadership skills. It is possible for a person to learn to "behave" like a leader, which is actually based mostly on learning what things to "do" as a leader (which we are calling leadership "tasks") and it is possible for a person to learn the skills required to lead. Acquiring both of these are independent of a natural, or innate, ability, or personality "trait," or what we are calling "behavior." However, if someone possesses an innate leadership trait, it will cause that person to gravitate, long before you come across him or her in your workforce, to leadership behavior. These are the children that you see on the playground leading the recess activities. There's a lot of truth to that old saying "I learned everything I needed to know in life on the kindergarten playground."

Moving on …

The natural leadership trait can give someone with leadership aspirations an advantage over the second person who wants to be a leader, but doesn't possess the trait (which leads to the behavior, which leads to the skills, which leads to the tasks) innately. However! If the person with the natural leadership trait, which caused the development of early leadership behavior, does not pursue learning the proven best practice skills of leadership (e.g., creating a vision, inspiring followership, oral and written communication,) then that natural leader will only progress to a certain point. Let's say, for the sake of comparison, that the natural ability will lead him past mediocrity, to a success level of 6 on a 10 point scale. Adding the leadership skills takes him to a success level of 10, but he neglects to see the value in these due to a successful track record (but remember, it's only a "6",) so he only learns some of them through exposure, and consequently only ever reaches a success level of 8.

Now let's consider the person who is not a natural leader but desires the role. While he may start out with a low natural ability, trial and error in life prior to joining your workforce will still probably get him to a success factor of 4. If his drive to lead is high enough, then he will apply himself to learning to such a degree that he spends a significant amount of time and energy learning to acquire the skills of leadership. With this diligence, he can expect to reach a success level of a 7 or 8.

Did you catch my between-the-lines suggestion? I've looked at this for many years in the laboratory of the real-world workforce, and I've concluded that those with a natural ability ("trait") for a particular job or role will, if they apply themselves to also learn the best practice skills for that job or role, they will surpass those without natural ability who are trying just as hard to acquire the skills. Like it or not, and it does rub against the grain of our modern "everyone is equal" thinking, but like it or not, natural traits pay off.

However!! What all this should tell us is that it is supremely important to help someone find his/her niche in the workforce!!!! When your informed recruiting meets your informed development program, success is imminent! We can still help those who want to move into areas outside of their natural ability, but all the better if we can help them migrate in the workforce towards that which does come natural, and then build onto that foundation the skills and knowledge, and other behaviors, that lead to job task ability, and hence success.

There is absolutely a powerful link between the job tasks you want done in the workplace to the type of behaviors you recruit for. If you find someone with the innate behavior, you significantly reduce the time to mastery, and also increase the eventual mastery level from a potential of 7 or 8 to a potential of 10.

Ok, get busy decomposing your company's job tasks into the component skills, knowledge, and behaviors! Then we can go fishing for our right candidates . . .

Now that we've talked about how the business world defines and uses jobs and job tasks in order to create, deliver, and sustain the goods and services the company wants to sell, we need to see how P.E.R.F.O.R.M. enables the Workforce Optimization practitioner to more easily manage this relationship.

Jobs and Job Tasks

P.E.R.F.O.R.M. catalogs both the jobs performed at a company AND the tasks performed in those jobs. In case you haven't picked up on the design strategy, when something can be used many times, such as one task can potentially be performed by many jobs, like answering the telephone (correctly, and hence the need for etiquette training, or something like that) P.E.R.F.O.R.M. will let you catalog those items in a list somewhere and then select from that list when you need to use it. This design strategy is what later will let you conduct many of the analysis features that make P.E.R.F.O.R.M. such a valuable business tool. This is the case for tying tasks to specific jobs, but we'll see how this works in just a moment. So then what about these Job Tasks? As we saw in the previous section where we discussed these business elements, jobs, as part of the company's Organizational Development efforts that result in a design of the jobs needed within the company in order to create, deliver, and sustain the goods and services that company wants to offer. P.E.R.F.O.R.M. let's you first catalog what all of those jobs are (each one is a separate record in the jobs table) and then the tasks and key aspects of each job. Some of the key things you'll want to capture (so you can use the tool to manage and tweak later) are:

- What is the job.
- What tasks are performed by someone doing the job.
- What specific Performance Measurements are used to evaluate success of someone doing the tasks performed in this job.
- What areas of the company have this job (e.g., each Dept. may have a "Sales" job)
- Required Learning for the job (e.g., a specific class)

- Questions to be used in an interview of someone for the job.
- Any specific things that enable someone to succeed at this job.
- The accountability factors to which someone in this job will be held.

The Job Tasks form lets you capture all of this data. To better understand the mechanics of this, let's take a look at the Job Tasks form.

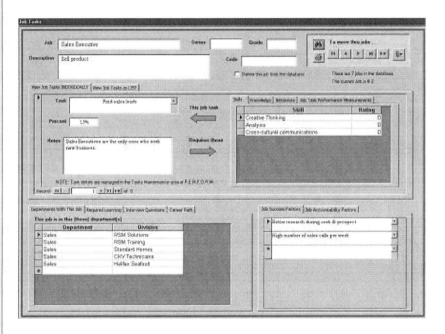

P.E.R.F.O.R.M. Screen– Job Tasks

Remember the "reusability" design factor behind P.E.R.F.O.R.M. Since one task might be performed by more than one job, and there is a lot of detail to each task (e.g., skills, knowledge, & behaviors, and task performance measurements) there is another area that lets you define each task, and then the center section of this Job Tasks form lets you "connect" the tasks to the jobs that do them.

The various tabs found in the bottom section of the Job Tasks form let you "connect" and/or create other elements that relate to this job. Each tab is described in the Fields, Buttons, and Tabs grid below.

Here is an explanation of the fields, buttons, and tabs on this form:

Item Name	What It's For
Job	Just as you'd guess, this is the name the company uses to refer to the job.
Series	Mostly for government agency use, but this can be used to classify the job.
Code	Mostly for government agency use, but this can be used to classify the job.
Description	I think of this as a place to describe the general purpose of the job.
Delete	Check box to use if you no longer want this entry. On a regular basis, the P.E.R.F.O.R.M. Systems Analyst will purge all items flagged by a user for deletion.
Task List Section	Each task is cataloged in the Tasks area, along with the Skills, Knowledge, and Behaviors needed to perform the task. In this section, the user simply selects a task by clicking the arrow to the right of the Task field pick-list. When a task is selected from the list, all of it's corresponding data is displayed in the details to the right.
Task List Section: Function	Additional information specific to this task for this job. Once the task is chosen, the user can identify the job function for which this is a part. Later, job definitions can be printed and/or analyzed, and this data element helps.
Task List Section: Percent of Time Spent	Additional information specific to this task for this job. Once the task is chosen, the user can identify the percentage of the total time taken up by this job task. While highest priority tasks do not always need or receive the highest percentage of time, this at least lets someone know how much time should be spent on this task in this job.

Required Learning
Interview Questions
Career Path
Job Success Enablers
Job Accountability Factors
Skills
Knowledge
Behaviors
Job Task Performance Measurements

The left margin shows a series of vertical tabs (reading bottom to top): Required Learning | Interview Questions | Career Path | Job Success Enablers | Skills | Knowledge | Job Accountability Factors | Behaviors | Job Task Performance Measurements

Task List Section: Job Task Performance Measurement	Additional information specific to this task for this job. Once the task is chosen, the user can identify one or more specific measurements used to look at the success of this job task. If we're going to design our Workforce Optimization strategy properly, we need to be able to analyze the performance that matters, and this link creates one of those important analysis keys.
Related Factor Section	This section connects and/or catalogs information pertinent to the job.
Related Factor Section: Departments With This Job tab	That's right, the Departments list is kept elsewhere, but here is where you identify which departments within the company have this job position.
Related Factor Section: Required Learning tab	A pick list once again. Use this if you want to mandate that someone in this job successful complete some class or other learning activity.
Related Factor Section: Interview Questions tab	Here we get a new type of list. This is both a pick list and a data entry field. If you have already created an interview question to ask for another job, that question will be in the pick list. If you want to create a new question, you simply type the new one at the bottom of the list. You can print an interview guide for the job based on the questions on this tab. The question will only appear on the guide if it is checkmarked.
Related Factor Section: Career Path tab	Create the jobs that this one allows someone to be ready for by picking those jobs from the list.
Related Factor Section: Job Success Enablers tab	A pick list or new data entry catalog of things some-one should do if he/she wants to be successful in the job. These things "enable" success. The explanation column is pretty important to help someone grasp the "why" and "how", so be sure to complete that too.

| Related Factor Section: Job Accountability Factors tab | Pretty similar in function to the last tab, but this one catalogs the things someone doing this job will be held accountable to achieve. If a Sales person needs to make 60 sales calls per month, here's where that gets documented. The Accountability Factors are later used in the Accountability Review area to auto-populate a review form. The form can then be edited to add/remove items, but this list forms the basis for the items to check during an accountability review (which is different than a performance review, which you'll see if you read that section . . .) |

Note - Employee Reviews and the corresponding Development Goals and Action Plans are all detailed in the section entitled *Performance and Accountability Reviews.*

Job Tasks and Learning Outcomes

In reality, job tasks become our Course Learning Outcomes. I won't revisit the importance of designing training with measurable outcomes, I'll instead refer you to the library of information you'll find on the subject. I'll summarize here with the conclusion that we know that good learning outcomes are those which center around the concept of what the event is intended to enable the learner to be able to **DO**. At the onset of my degree work in Instructional Systems Design, in ISD 101, we spent several hours going over the DO concept and memorizing the learning outcome mantra "At the end of this learning event, the person will be able to (fill in the verb describing what the learner will be able to do.)"

Since I was already employed full-time as I was working through my Masters program, I was able to immediately apply what I was learning. What I found was more of the same struggle brought on by job competencies. Once again, it may just be my limited ability, but I really found it painful to come up with these Learning Outcomes as I was thinking of training courses intended to help teach an IT person how to monitor and troubleshoot production runs of computer programs. It quickly dawned on me that they were an added layer to define before I could get into what I believed was the real purpose of the training.

I hate to admit my neglect of such a hallmark of my ISD foundation, but it wasn't too long before I found myself waiting to write the learning outcomes for the lesson plans last. I was still faithfully writing them on the whiteboard at the start of each class, but I was already starting to think of them as "overhead" when I was designing the courseware. Even though I knew from my graduate studies that the single factor of telling a group what the learning outcomes are at the start of the education increases learning transfer by 3%, I still didn't like doing it. It just seemed to be "HR-speak" and created distance between the group and me. I liked having learning objectives, even though I thought of them as "extra work," but I really didn't like having to announce them.

Then one day the two worlds collided.

I was in the midst of working with the shift I supervised, discussing the steps we used to store computer backup tapes (we were mired in the happy task of writing procedures manuals at the time) when it struck me. The reason we were trying to document these process steps was so that someone could follow the procedure to do the task, and that was the same basic purpose of a learning event, to enable someone to be able to do the steps involved in performing a job task. Why not just make that the Learning Outcome of the learning events – to be ABLE TO DO a specific job task. We already had the tasks defined in the process flows, so we could easily reuse them as the learning outcome statements. Problem solved!

OK, maybe you're not impressed, but it was like lightening to me!

We'll discuss later how the ability to do a task is dependent on enabling skills, knowledge, and/or behaviors, and developing those in someone will be the enabling learning objectives of your learning events. For example, someone may need to know how to read a tape measure in order to cut a board to a certain length. Reading the tape measure is an enabling skill to the learning outcome (and I should add: "job task in the real world".) In fact, within your "reading a tape measure" enabling skill is another level of enabling skills, working with fractions, or basic mathematics. If you are running a training function, then it would be wise to collect as much details on these job tasks, and all of the enablers, and then attack at the level of reusability, such as some learning media that teaches basic math. More on this later …

The key here is to realize that we shouldn't reinvent learning outcomes over in the Training side of the business, but rather use the job tasks already defined by the business units to be the learning objectives of the learning events.

> ### Higher Job Performance Results Come From Aggregate Planning
>
> Good job design = tasks + motivational fit + fast track mastery. In other words, as you work with the business unit managers to design the jobs and job tasks, think about what mastery you can borrow from the readily available workforce, and what elements can be added to the job that tap into readily available motivating elements.
>
> Maybe this is better explained by using an example. During the days of the Gulf War, I was amazed at the technology behind the very effective "smart bombs." As the Evening News anchor explained how the soldiers guided the bombs to their targets with pinpoint precision, I was quickly struck by the similarities to the guidance system technology and the old video games that many young Americans grew up with. The designers of those systems were able to leverage an existing skill set, with all of its familiarity, to fast-track mastery of their missile guidance technology. Imagine the learning curve they'd face if we didn't have the benefit of a lifetime of training youth through video games. It also has the seeds of a new conspiracy theory . . .
>
> Now I have no idea or insight into how those two worlds came together, but we can at least learn a powerful lesson from it, whether it was intentional upfront or just a lucky break. The lesson I took from that experience was that, from that time forward, whenever I was trying to help improve the efficiency of a business unit through better job design, I always asked myself the question "is there something we can borrow from the life experience of the average employee to make this job have elements that are either familiar to them or appealing. Even if the job tasks take 10% longer to perform, or it adds 10% more steps, if the job has a faster learning curve or a higher level of engagement, the cumulative effect will be greater performance levels.

Job Performance Measurement

There will always be a need to understand how well an employee performs his/her job. To answer this need, unfortunately, many companies jump to the quick and easy solution. While it's not a core component of Workforce Optimization, job design is a piece of the performance puzzle, so it merits looking at for a moment.

Whenever possible, challenge yourself, as you manage job design, to build processes and tasks into the design of the job that not only makes it easier or more efficient to do the job, but that will also feed into an easier way to gauge job performance. This concept is probably best understood through an example.

Let's use our Sales person case study. A key result a company looks for in a good Salesperson is not just growing the customer base, but improving the <u>quality</u> of the customer base. So now then how do we determine if a Sales person is nailing this element of high job performance? How does the Sales person's boss know if he/she is closing **good** business? Here's where good job design will pay off. Let's consider our options:

> **Option 1**) use a subjective measurement which would require the boss or the Sales person, or someone, to evaluate a customer's "goodness" level and render a rating.

> **Option 2**) build objective measurements into the job design, such as defining "good" business as those customers who make repeat purchases, have a low number of problems, or whatever equals "goodness."

If we choose option 1, then someone will have to do additional work in order to gauge job performance. As well, it's a subjective measurement, which is always a shaky ground on which to found analysis.

However, if we choose option 2, then it will take some work upfront to define what "good" means, and it may take some time to create a tool that helps the company efficiently keep track of problems, or know when a customer makes a repeat purchase, but those tools will drive efficiency in the job, and then also be usable to measure job performance.

Having a good way to objectively measure job performance will pay off later when we use it to identify top performers and also evaluate the level

> **Workforce Optimization Maxim #2: Never add work in order to measure work**

training delivers in terms of job impact. This is a great example of **Workforce Optimization Maxim #2: never add work in order to measure work.**

EVERYTHING is a part of job performance. If we have to add a factor that inhibits job performance in order to be able to measure job performance, then what good have we really done? Think of it as the company that wants to know the level of customer satisfaction. Option 1: customer survey. How many companies have customer surveys? Just this week I made a purchase at a major department store (as I write this it's Christmas shopping season) and my register receipt had a toll free number I could call and answer an automated survey. To get me to give up my time for their survey, the store was offering me a two dollar coupon after I finished the phone call. I decided to do without the two bucks.

My point is that it would be better for them to have challenged themselves to figure out option 2: build a way to check customer satisfaction into their job design. How about repeat customers? If nothing else, this can be determined as a byproduct of credit card purchases. You could very easily get a statistic of how many repeat credit card customers you have.

The same challenge applies to job performance. If we challenge ourselves, we can figure out how to design an element into the job that will enable us, as some sort of byproduct, to evaluate job performance. Don't make your employees fill out cards or checkmark boxes or do any other extra piece of work only so you can use it later for measuring. There are plenty of ways to build measurements into an efficiency/effectiveness element of a job's tasks.

While we're in the neighborhood, I might as well introduce the third maxim we'll try to store away. Think of it as trying to keep the bigger picture clearly in focus when you build and/or adjust the little pieces of the puzzle. If you prefer a rugged outdoors analogy: "remember you're growing a forest whenever you plant and/or prune each individual tree." The challenge of this book is to explain the finer points of the individual areas or components of performance while

> **Workforce Optimization Maxim #3: Always keep the big picture in view.**

at the same time trying to explain how they work in concert with each other. At times it will be more important to lose a little in terms of an individual area in order to make it serve the larger good of the whole environment. I'll try to point this out as we discuss each of the components.

Whose Turf Is It Anyway?

Lest I mislead you into thinking that Workforce Optimization is merely a matter of recruiting, hiring, and training, let me broaden the horizon. Consider the company that needs to have one or more departments available 24 hours a day, 7 days a week. To answer this need, most companies adopt the post-WWII model of three shifts, each working eight hours, and then some iteration of coverage over the weekend. I worked in just such a department some years ago, so this example is direct from the real world. We found ourselves in a situation where we had many employees working overtime each week in order to provide weekend coverage and turnover time from one shift to another. The problem intensified due to what we perceived as run-away sick leave. In a first step towards a self-directed work-team approach, the management team offered to let those of us in the department come up with ideas for how to solve the problem.

In true Yeoman fashion, we put our heads together and came up with a radical new idea: change the shift structure. We determined that four shifts working 13 hours per day but for only 3 days per shift, could provide us ample coverage for the hours that needed to be staffed. I should clarify that there was work that started on each Friday night, carried through all day on Saturday, and concluded sometime

---

New Shift Structure

Shift One: Mon, Tues, & Wed days, 7:00 am – 8:00 pm.

Shift Two: Mon, Tues, & Wed nights, 7:00 pm – 8:00 am.

Shift Three: Thurs, Fri, & Sat days, 7:00 am – 8:00 pm.

Shift Four: Thurs, Fri, & Sat nights, 7:00 pm – 8:00 am

---

on Saturday's wee hours of the morning, which most people refer to as Sunday morning. There was rarely a need for the shop to be open past 8:00 am Sunday morning. The proposal was adopted by the management team, and did, in fact, yield the results we expected: overtime was almost completely eliminated. What's more, each day shift overlapped with the night shift for one hour in the first and second evening and morning, and then with the next shift on Wednesday. There was more consistent information sharing across all shifts due to the overlap.

But now for the unexpected outcome . . .

After a month or two of the new schedule, we noticed an interesting change in employee performance. We had fewer sick leave outages, (sick leave went down from 6 average outages per employee per year down to 2!!) and also less work errors (error rates went down from 14 errors average per shift down to 3, and for some periods of time even 0!!) When we looked into the cause, we found that people felt that they could better balance their work and personal lives, and, even though their "work shift days" left little time for personal matters, the four "off days" more than made up for it. Their job performance was higher because they were able to focus more on their job requirements at hand when it was their time to be "on the job."

Now I'm not out to advocate we all change to 3 day work weeks (although for some positions we found that four 10-hour days were more productive than five 8-hour days!.) What I am after here is to use a real-world example to illustrate

> **Workforce Optimization Maxim #4: If it affects job performance, I need to understand it!**

my point. So what's my point? That Workforce Optimization practitioners need to be aware of, AND MANAGE, any and all of the factors that lead to enhanced job performance or inhibits job performance. If you have the true spirit of partnership and a desire to help, the business unit will welcome the insight into all matters related to job performance. If you have a "lord it over others" spirit, well, you may as well stop reading here, because I don't want to be a party to the lynching . . .

Here is a real-world example of the two primary factors that affect an employee's job performance: ability and desire. You can think of desire as deeply affected by attitude. In the case of our 13 hours a day, 3-day work week structure, there was a marked increase in job performance simply because the employees were happier with their weekly schedule. We set out to reduce overtime cost and ended up learning an important lesson in how to affect job performance. In some ways, it was the start of what to date is what you're reading here!

By the way, there was maximum buy-in for the shift structure change on the part of the department employees because we had come up with the idea in the first place. Just thought I'd put in a plug for not only the problem solving potential of the average employee, but also the value of enabling people to have a voice in shaping their own environment. That's another small ingredient in the Workforce Optimization recipe: **involvement**.

Measuring Learning Success

Remember way back when we started our discussions, the key questions we said need to be answered by the Human Resources Management area, and especially the Workforce Optimization practitioner? One of those questions is "How do I spend my training dollars?" It's time to start answering that question. The simple answer is "spend them on the learning activities that have the greatest effect on job performance." But that answer begins the journey it doesn't end it! If that's the answer to the first question, then it only leads me to ask "how do I know what learning activities result in the greatest effect on job performance?" What we need to know, and trust me, there's a way to answer that, is how can we determine what learning activities produce both individual and collective results. In other words, I need to know if each person has learned something, and I need to know if what they learned made a difference in the results of the job they do.

Another huge reward of using job tasks to define the learning outcomes is when we reach the point of designing the success criteria and measurements for a learning event. Once again, a payoff from the era of Total Quality Management, we learned that if you want to improve a job process you have to be able to measure a job process. The age of process measurement was born! As well, every job in every company has its output measurements that the company uses to gauge the performance level of the individual worker.

Put those measurements on the table, and now mix it with what we've learned about measuring learning success. As before, I won't revisit all of the great literature we already have on this subject, but I will suggest a thorough reading of Donald L. and James D. Kirkpatrick's book entitled *Evaluating Training Programs: The Four Levels, Third Edition*. While others may also have elaborated on how to measure the success of a learning activity, he was the first I encountered, and I find myself returning time and again to how he recommends we evaluate training success. Forgive me if I err by summarizing, but I like to think of Donald and James Kirkpatrick's four stages of measurement as:

1. Did the learners think it was worthwhile? (usually a class survey)
2. Is the level of ability higher? (usually the pre- and post-tests)
3. Is job performance levels higher? (job impact)
4. Did higher job performance impact job results? (work impact)

Being a die hard business unit manager, I'll cut to the chase: I really only worry about levels three and four. As an ISD practitioner, I realize the need to be able to prove, through level two checking, that the class accomplished what it was intended to accomplish, but what really matters in business is did it get any tangible results.

If, as part of our Workforce Optimization efforts, we define, capture, or somehow document the measurements the business units already have in place to gauge employee job performance, and if we use the job tasks to design our learning activities around, then it is a short step to get to meaningful ways to measure the success of our learning activities. We can reuse the job performance measurements as indicators of the success or failure of a learning activity. Not only is it an efficient approach since we won't need to create an added layer of job measurement that must be fed to be used, we are taking our cue directly from the same metrics the company holds to be useful.

Time For A "Real World" Case Study

If a learning event is designed to help a Salesperson better identify good sales prospects, and the company is already measuring the ratio of leads to closed accounts, then the gauge of the success of the learning activity is how much it affected the close ratio measurement. After the learning activity, did the person's ratio improve? "Yes"? Maybe it was the learning activity. "No"? Maybe the learning is not helpful. Keep in mind, I'm being vague in both directions because we also know that improvement or lack thereof is not due entirely to the learning activity. If we see things get better, we can make a strong argument that it is due to good instruction design and execution, but it's best to wait until we have the results in greater number before we give a round of high-fives and fist-bumps. More on that subject is elsewhere in this recipe book . . .

I'd like to highlight the measurable difference that tying training to job performance had in this real-world case study. When employees attended training without a direct tie, there was a 15% "no show" percentage for learning events. When the connection to job performance was tracked and publicized, there was a 3% "no show" percentage. There were still people who missed the event, but this is always going to be the case. At least it went to a more manageable percentage.

An intangible benefit, but one that I personally enjoyed maybe even more, was the increase in the respect level from the management tier. As the approach became more "scientific" the management team took more of an interest. When asked, most of them told me that it seemed more businesslike with this approach! Whatever! It is, and I liked the results, so that gave me one more reason to take this "tie it to the money" approach.

How Does P.E.R.F.O.R.M. Support This?

Ok, you've seen the ability of P.E.R.F.O.R.M. to help you manage the data, and present it as information, that enables you to see the tie from the business results, to the measurements that gauge them, to the jobs where people do things to bring about the desired results, now we get into how P.E.R.F.O.R.M. helps you look at and manage the tie to what is done in employee development to enable people to do the job tasks that lead to the optimum performance.

When we record an employee's information, one of the things we identify there is his/her current job. With that accomplished, we have now tied a person to his/her direct performance measurements, but also to his/her job tasks (with their tie to the same list of measurements) through the relationship to his/her job. But there's still one more piece to this part of the P.E.R.F.O.R.M. support of the Workforce Optimization puzzle. The direct tie of a Learning Activity to these performance measurements.

In the catalog of Learning Activities, P.E.R.F.O.R.M. lets you define any life experience, especially Training Classes, and their corresponding Learning Outcomes by choosing them from a list of all the job tasks. Because we have job tasks in the database already, it's very easy to then define a learning activity by the job tasks it enables someone to perform. As you choose one or more job task to be a learning outcome of the learning activity (boy, that's a lot of learning going on ...) you will automatically have tied a participant in a session of that learning activity to the job task for the event (I got tired of the word "learning activity" myself, so I switched to "event".)

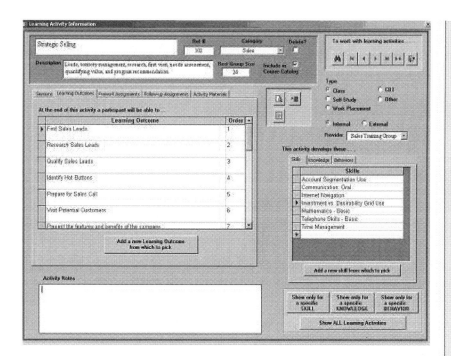

P.E.R.F.O.R.M. Screen– Learning Activity Information

Since we already have the job tasks in P.E.R.F.O.R.M. as a result of defining jobs, to add them as the learning outcomes in the Learning Activities catalog is as simple as picking them from a drop-down list!

As we later check the benefit of a Learning Activity, such as a training class, we'll determine if it is a worthwhile class based on its job impact as reflected in the real-world company measurement tied to the job tasks that the course was intended to enable. If the results of people who participate in a session of a learning activity, probably checked using the Peer To Peer form, have job performance measurements that have gone up, **based on the real world data metric** used by the company, we'll know that our learning activity probably contributed, and is therefore probably sound, at least for this session of it for these participants (keeping in mind our rule that no one factor creates or inhibits success.) If there's no movement, then we may have a course that isn't as worthwhile as we thought, or we may have a bad management support plan (the things we plan to have happen before, during, and after the learning activity.)

Here is an explanation of the fields, buttons, and tabs on the Learning Activity form:

Item Name	What It's For
Title	The name the company uses to refer to this activity.
Include In Course Catalog	You can print a report that includes the details of any event where this checkbox has been set to "on"
Sessions Tab	Every iteration of this event. There is a another form that shows all sessions of all events. This also controls what choices appear in the related two Registration Forms.
Learning Outcomes	This is where each job task that the event enables gets selected. There is no limit to how many can be associated to a single learning event.
"This activity enables these … Skills, Knowledge, & Behaviors" section	When a person completes a learning event, you can choose to credit that person with all of the s,k,&b's associated with the learning event. This will add them to their personal catalog for use later in selecting the right candidates for a job opening, and also for their own Career Planning using P.E.R.F.O.R.M.

Chapter Five:
The Building Blocks of Workforce Optimization

- Into the Planning War Room

- Some Thoughts On Attitude Adjustment

Into The Planning War Room

Workforce Optimization, as I wrote a minute ago is the result of taking many disparate parts and using them in aggregate. It's going to take this whole book to unpack all of them, but I'm going to start here, and we'll build as we go. We need to assemble all of the ingredients in the recipe before we start to cook our feast, but let's spend a few sentences on explaining the nature of the dishes we're going to be serving.

Where can we say is the start and end of a perfect circle? Therein lies the dilemma of this cookbook. How can I help you build when that has to be done over time, and time locks us into a linear process. That's why I've chosen the analogy of relating this to a chef who needs to serve a multi-course meal. If we've taken the time to understand the whole meal, which we did in the first few chapters, then now it's time to roll up our sleeves and walk into the kitchen. Or do we go into the dining room first and scope out the seating arrangements … Or do we need to survey the people who are going to dine first … starting to see the problem?

Here's how I'm going to try to get us past this sloth of despair. Just like a chef, think of our strategy as:
1. plan everything first (which you've already begun by reading this book!),
2. start all of the major dishes at the same time,
3. give attention to key elements of each main dish in its turn,
4. start the secondary dishes when it's time for them,
5. bring some things to the front burner for awhile, some things to the back,
6. serve the first course when it's time, while still preparing the others,
7. serve each course as it's due,
8. when all is done, enjoy the results, and then start over for the next day's meal.

Did you catch the core component of managing the process? Knowing and executing the timing of what gets attention when. Of course you still have to know how to prepare each dish, but the art of the Master Chef is knowing how to put all of the dishes together to create a fine dining experience. Anyone can master one or two dishes, not many can become the Master Chef.

We'll get into each one of these, but let me give you the quick-hit list of the steps to implementing a Workforce Optimization program at a company:

1. Define company goals & performance metrics.
2. Define jobs: job tasks, and task skills, knowledge, and behaviors.
3. Develop training courses for job task s/k/b's.
4. Supervisors learn and use coaching for performance.
5. Employees use Best Practice's for self-learning.
6. Offer courses for job task development.
7. Employees learn and use Career Planning for self-assessment.
8. Workforce Optimization Analysts use comparison tools to identify job performance enhancing factors.

Soooo … Into the Planning War Room

That's right, not the kitchen or the dining room, but the planning room, wherever that is for you. Maybe it's a public workshop for Workforce Optimization, maybe it's your normal office, maybe you have to go to the beach or the mountains. Wherever and whatever it is, it's time to plan our attack.

First off, let's agree that what we're after is optimal employee performance. To me, that means getting the best performance possible out of someone with the least amount of "ramp up" time. The goal is to achieve an employee who is fully engaged in his or her job. In order to begin to understand this concept of a "fully engaged employee," let's take a quick minute to lay some Workforce Optimization foundation. We'll spend more time on this "fully engaged employee" in subsequent sections, but for now, we need a platform from which to get a few things out on the table . . .

Firstly, for an employee to function at his/her ultimate capacity, he/she must be committed and connected to his/her job to the highest degree possible. He (I got tired of writing he/she, so please interpret "he" to be a universal generic reference without resorting to using the word "it") needs to be able to do his job in all aspects from an ability perspective, but he also has to **want** to do his job to his highest ability from a motivation perspective. It is of little value to have a highly skilled person if he doesn't really want to work, and it is of little value either to have someone who truly wants to do a great job but lacks skills and/or knowledge necessary to actually do what the job requires. Ultimately, you need both *Attitude* and *Ability*.

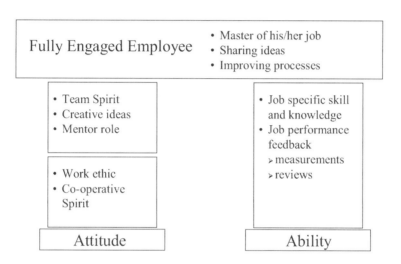

If you have the admirable intentions to help people to realize their highest job potential, and to help the workforce as a whole to achieve maximum business results, then you must investigate and intervene in both areas that affect performance. To neglect one or the other will have mitigating influence on the overall potential.

For most of this book, I'm going focus on the *Ability* side of the equation. As we get into this discussion, we'll look at the factors that influence results. Keep in mind, these "influencers" will impact both ability and attitude, so as we talk about them within the ability focus, we're also learning about things that influence the attitude element as well.

There are basically two groupings of these performance influencers: things done as part of doing the job itself (the job;) and things done more specific to the people and specific persons in the job (the people.) They are at the same time inter-related within their "group" and intra-related to the other "group". In other words, one thing done for "the job" will impact the other things that are specific to the job itself, and the collection of things done for "the job" will cause things to be more or less effective with the group of things done that are specific to the people and specific persons who do the job. As well, one thing done with "the people" will impact the other things done with people doing the job, and the collection of things done with "the people" will cause things done for "the job" to be more or less effective.

For example, within the group of things done with the people and persons who do the job, if we recruit someone who has a better intrinsic fit for the behaviors necessary to succeed in the job, then we will need to spend less time in the subsequent accountability reviews doing things to motivate and/ or moderate his behavior in the job. He'll have higher "motivational fit" with his job, and will therefore require less attitude intervention. One of the things done within the group of influencers on the people side of the house has now had an impact on another thing done on the people side of the house. As well, because these two items, when later combined, have fostered a more highly engaged employee, the effect that has on the group of influencers germane to the job itself, we'll call it the business side of the house, is that now we will need fewer employees in order to achieve an output level. Things done on the people side of the house has now had an effect on the business side of the house.

Ultimately, if we are to achieve optimal workforce performance, and optimal individual performance within that, we need to address both sides of the performance equation: influencers grouped as pertaining to the job itself, and influencers grouped as pertaining to the people and individual persons who do the jobs. We need to have well designed jobs within well-defined functional areas, and we need skilled individual employees within a skilled (and peacefully cohabitating) workforce.

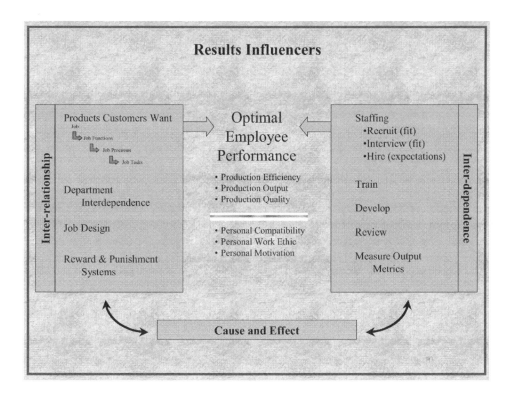

Some Thoughts On Attitude Adjustments

Work attitude is very tenuous ground to explore, and one where perhaps the ART of applying the science of Workforce Optimization comes more to bear, but it's one we must discuss if we are to have the full picture of factors that contribute and/or inhibit workplace results. I wish I could be more Polly Anna about this subject, but I'd rather take what I'd call a more "realistic" perspective when I evaluate employees' attitudes. What I've found through the years in the HR field is that most people would rather be spending their time somewhere other than "at work." At best I'll agree that it's a 50-50 split on this for people "in the trenches," although analysis tells me that our old friend Pareto has this ratio more closely tuned in: about 80% of the workforce would rather be somewhere else, while about 20% are intrinsically engaged. They'll still do their job, because they have to, but the questions remain:

1. "What sort of attitude do they have while doing their job?"
2. "What negative affect has attitude had on quantity and quality?"
3. "How can we help them have a better attitude?"

The 80/20 ratio does begin to reverse as you analyze higher in the organization structure. The ratio reversal is only partially based on compensation (28%), partly based on the interest level of the tasks performed at higher levels (34%), and partly (38%) on the nature of people who rise into the executive ranks. Since the majority of the people we will need to work with if we are to optimize the workforce is part of the potentially "attitude challenged" group, (80% of the 80% who comprise the bulk of the workforce,) we need to have strategies and techniques to stimulate higher/better/healthier employee attitudes, both individually and corporately. The good news is that there are ways to create an atmosphere that fosters collective "positive attitudes" and techniques of working with individuals that will keep individual employee attitudes higher. There will always be the "rotten apples in the barrel," but we can move into place ideas and practices that will keep this group to a manageable less-than-5% number.

Reality check: No one I know or ever heard of works "on task" 100% of his workday time, therefore I believe it's not done because it can't be done. I'm not saying people are innately lazy, but I am saying that people tend to interact with others, and have personal "wandering off" time, as part of their human natures. So it's not the goal of Workforce Optimization to drive this out of the work environment, but rather to help employee's have the best possible attitude so they stay "on task" as much as possible, and to build their ability so that when they are on task they achieve the highest possible productivity results.

If you want to help your employees with their attitudes, then I suggest we talk for a moment about life circumstances and their effect on employee attitude. Essentially, all motivation in the workplace can be traced to its connection with something personal. There are things that you can do that are not ability development related that will affect someone's attitude, such as awarding someone a raise. A good raise is always a way to boost their attitude, and hence boost their output (I'm not taking about the quality of the output, only quantity, although quality may go up because they WANT to do a better job and so apply the skills they've had all along to a higher level.) Career opportunities are also a good way to "motivate" someone, which is a good way to think about what I'm suggesting as we talk about attitude.

94   THE BUILDING BLOCKS OF WORKFORCE OPTIMIZATION

We're hoping to stimulate the best attitude, and that is often referred to as "motivating" someone. HOWEVER, even though these factors are workplace centered, they are ultimately tied to something that motivates someone at the personal level. Maybe the career opportunities stimulate a positive attitude because the employee sees potential future financial gains, or maybe they just like to think of themselves as a future more "important person" in the company, and that motivates them. Whatever the reason, it's still tied to something personal. So, if a company wants to help someone have a better workplace attitude, the company needs to have a work environment that helps people fulfill the fundamental drive for personal benefit. Once again, it's not all financial. Personal benefit for some people takes the shape of career advancement potential. For others it is task challenge. For others it is involvement in decision making. For others it is, well, I'll come back to this when we close out this section on attitude adjustments.

In addition to those things that the company can directly do to affect attitude, there are life circumstances that need to be understood as to their effect on employee attitude. Later in this recipe book we'll talk more at length about these Miscellaneous Factors that have a cause and effect relationship on employee attitude, but I want to get the seeds planted now so you can keep them in mind as we talk more about what can be done to affect ability. Remember, it's the **dual support platform of Ability and Attitude** that result in optimum performance!

Ok, so consider this, an employee is thinking of making some large scale purchase in his/her life. Maybe it's a home, a car, or maybe a boat. It can even be a nice vacation. In the weeks and months leading up to the purchase, his/her "personal wandering time" will be spent on thinking about what he/she wants to purchase, and even, sorry to say, talking with others about it. It's a factor of people in the workplace, and minimizing it while acknowledging its reality and need is a task of management. But anyway, back to our trying to understand its effect on attitude … As the employee thinks about making his/her large scale purchase, it is common to reflect on how the job has enabled that purchase. It could be an idealistic reflection ("Isn't it wonderful of the company to pay me enough that I can buy this _____!") or could be a practical/realistic reflection

("I need this job if I'm going to buy this _____ !") Either way, it makes the employee's attitude get better.

However, that does mean it lasts forever …

There is a period of time that varies by individual (my records show it is from 90 days to as long as 6 months) before the "bump" that comes from the purchase gives way to the "slump" that comes from not be able to enjoy the new purchase. The new "I want to be on my boat!" attitude sets in, and it's time for a new strategy.

I'm not trying to paint a negative picture of human motivation. Some people are more motivated around the reality of the necessity of work and finding jobs that they can enjoy. Others will need your help to turn this corner. For both of these, though, I'd say there are still things to consider which enhance attitude, and thusly make higher performing employees. Consider the work team that I wrote about earlier who changed to a three-day, 13-hour day work week. The company gained because overtime was eliminated. The employees gained because they had four days per week to pursue life interests. In that case, the initial motivation from making the change never went away. It did go down 6 months after the change, but was still 23% higher than attitude prior to the change.

In evaluating performance data from different companies for the last 15 years, I discovered the number one contributor to higher employee attitude (and culprit leading to lower attitude level, and the "cancer" of disgruntled employees) is the element of "**fairness**." In the eyes of the employee, performance stays at an acceptable level when the employee feels he/she has been treated "fairly." Now before you throw up your hands and despair or throw this recipe book out the window, let me define "fairness" in a way that is usable in a business setting.

My insight on the subject of perceived fairness is most accurately attributed to my experience as a middle school teacher (6th-8th grades) several years ago. After repeatedly hearing that I wasn't being "fair," I realized I needed a better working definition of "fair" for my classes and us to use in our dealings. "Fair" is most clearly understood as **the absence of surprises**. When we discussed acceptable and unacceptable performance, I was clear as to the results that would come from each. When performance was acceptable, I was obligated to apply the results I'd lead them to expect, and when the performance was unacceptable, I was also obligated to apply the results I'd lead them to expect. This forced me to become extremely more cautious as to what I told people I would and wouldn't do, particularly when it came to negative reinforcement, an area in which I'm a self-confessed pushover.

Can you guess where I'm going with this illustration?

In the workplace, we can greatly benefit from the use of this definition of "fair." When employees clearly understand performance expectations, and when they clearly understand results, and when – now here's the REAL key – when **performance discussions are based primarily (not entirely) on empirical data not subjective opinion**, THEN the percentage of employees who perceive their career handling as being "fair" goes up, and their corresponding job performance level stays in the acceptable range. An open and honest expectations discussion forces the employee to see himself as the captain of his career fate, working within a business reality that <u>must</u> produce financially viable results (remember back to the opening section of this book?) But this evaluation needs to be fact based, and we need to be ready to live up to what we lead the employee to expect, both positive and negative.

If you'll indulge me just this once, I want to have a brief summary of these points, because this attitude factor is somewhere in the neighborhood of 30% of the overall success potential (70% being the Ability side of the equation,) so we need to be sure we discuss it clearly. **Employee attitude is a combination of two primary influencers: perceived personal benefit and perceived fairness.** The underlying maxims of Workforce Optimization support the need, and enable the practice, of companies to create and foster a collective and individual environment for positive employee attitudes. As you implement the "little things" of Workforce Optimization, the "big things" of attitude and ability take care of themselves.

By the way, measuring attitude isn't done by sending out "employee satisfaction surveys." That might give you the information you're looking for, but it's questionable as to honesty, and it requires some administrative management and time for each person to complete the survey, a drain of some percentage on workplace output. Also, keep in mind, employee satisfaction surveys carry with them, intended or not, an implied agreement that the company will correct, not just address, any complaints that surface in the survey process. Probably not what you want to set your company up for. The way I'd suggest measuring employee attitude is to think about how high attitude levels manifest in job practices, and how low attitude levels manifest themselves. Here are some ideas for measuring employee attitude levels:

- new ideas for how to do job tasks (better attitudes will cause people to want to do the job better, and be willing to share those ideas)
- employee referrals of new employee candidates
- turnover (I think you can figure this one out …)
- sick leave (your peer group will have an average, those spiking higher are in the red zone)
- tenure (better attitudes lead to longer tenure)
- error rates (better attitudes lead to less errors)
- majority performing at acceptable levels

Oh! I want to talk later in detail about positive and negative results of performance, but just in case I forget to mention it later, **healthy reward systems** are a huge contributor to employee attitude. If you're trying to create reward systems, let me suggest the best way I've ever found for this: **ask the employees**. Do this one-to-one. Just ask various employees "What would you like to see/have in your workplace experience?" You'll definitely learn of creative and acceptable ideas that you never would have thought of. I did!! Repeatedly!!

Chapter Six:
Crossing Over

- Changing an Employee's Job Performance

- Performance and Accountability Reviews and Compensation

- Whose Job Is It Anyway?

- The Unknown Variables of Top Performance

Changing An Employee's Job Performance

I hope you haven't been deceived by our light-hearted approach into thinking that this isn't serious stuff! If so, then let me wave a flag for this topic and say firmly to you "focus." Here is where we get to the first of many payoff points. I want to introduce the first "big picture' integration junction between some of the elements that make up a Workforce Optimization environment. Up until now we've talked mostly about some of the individual trees. Now I'd like for us to step back for a moment, don't worry, we're headed back into the details in a moment, but let's stop for a moment, take a step back, and look at one of the panoramic views of our forest.

We've looked already at jobs and the business use of their processes, and later we'll get into designing and delivering learning activities targeted to job performance improvement, and we'll also talk in detail about employee reviews, but we can start even at this point to discuss tying employee growth plans directly to the business goals of the company. Let's start our discussion with a diagram.

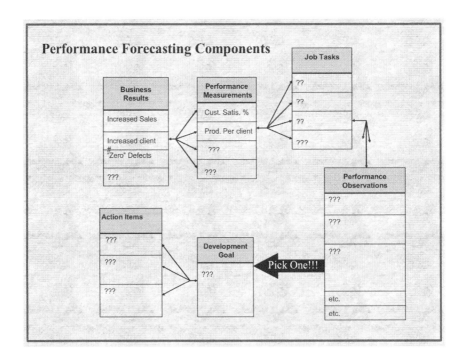

Take a look at the title for this illustration. Notice anything? It's not 'Workforce Optimization" it's "Performance Forecasting." What management interests are trying to understand is what performance level can we expect from certain people, given specific history, job structure, and interventions. In a sense, we are trying to predict, or "forecast," future performance. The underlying reality is that if we can predict future performance, then we would need to know the factors that result in that performance, and that gives us the "stuff" we need to then optimize the performance. As we learn about the background and environment that fosters top performers, we will also be learning what profile to look for initially that will result in top future performers, and the interventions we'll need to make over time to stimulate growth towards top performance.

How we manage those interventions is what the diagram is attempting to illustrate. Starting from the top left, we see that as a company identifies the business results it wants to achieve, it will also move into place measurements to gauge the level of those desired results. Knowing that, it is a short step, for each measurement, to identify the jobs, and more specifically the job **tasks**, that affect each measurement.

In the diagram, the business result example is the desire of the company to increase its number of customers. For the goal of increasing the number of customers, this company has moved into place the measurements of the percent (%) level of customer satisfaction, the number of products per client, and probably some others (hence the triple questions marks.) What this illustrates is that this company believes that the % level of satisfied customers and the number of products per client indicates some reflection on how well they are working with their customers, and, if these measurements are good, the company can expect that its number of customers will increase (that is the goal we started with.) In other words, by focusing their attention on the two indicators (% level of satisfied customers and # of products,) as the company does things to affect those elements, that will lead to the goal they're after, more customers. That takes us to the next step of identifying ways to affect each of those measurements. The diagram takes us down the path of the # of Products Per Client.

The next link in the crossover chain is to look at the job tasks that people in the organization do that has some affect on this particular measurement. If the focus is on the number of products per client, then it stands to reason that in the function of Sales, one of the job tasks should be to introduce new and/or multiple products to each customer. As a Salesperson performs this job task, as it is performed more successfully, the result will be that the customer buys more products, and the resulting measurement is affected. If more products are explained to a customer, the number of people who will buy goes up based on the percentage of those who buy. If 10% of the potential customer group will buy one product from the company, then I can increase the odds that a product will appeal to them if I show then two products instead of just one, if I explain the two products in a way that appeals but doesn't overwhelm or confuse. But then again, that's an element of determining how to best perform a job task, which we'll get into later. For now, let's keep following the crossover chain . . .

If you look then at the next box, you'll see that, in the routine functions out in the trenches, a manager or coach is **observing** a person doing this job task. Job review is no longer for the sake of job review, it's job review around **a specific job task**, because increasing the performance of the job task has a direct link back to the key goal of the company, through the intervening performance 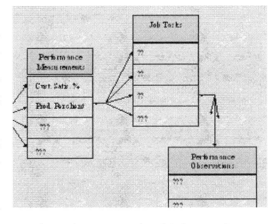 measurements. The better a person introduces new/multiple products to customers will affect the number of products purchased by those customers, and that will, in turn, accomplish the company goal of increasing the number of customers. When we get into how to handle employee job performance discussions, we'll look at best practice ideas for performance observation, the key thing to take away from this discussion is to realize that the observation is specific to a job task, and the time investment is prioritized because that task has been identified as one of the ones leading to higher results in a key area.

That's one example of "optimization." Spending time on those activities that achieve the maximum resulting impact.

About the diagram: if you look at how the diagram is structured, it's trying to illustrate that one item in a preceding box will most likely have multiple entries in a successive box. For example, the single item of "Products Per Client" in the Performance Measurements box was tied to, or affected by, multiple job tasks in the Job Tasks box. As well, someone doing a single job task might have multiple performance observations as to how well he/she is performing that single task. It's an ever-widening circle (I'll spare you the analogy about ponds and stones and all that …) but, once again, worth the effort because it's been identified proactively as a key area to improve in order to achieve the company's goals.

Don't panic! We'll get to, in a second, how P.E.R.F.O.R.M. will support this crossing over chain! For now, two more quick steps in the chain . . .

It is vital to Change Management effectiveness (yes, that's another ingredient in the Workforce Optimization recipe) that any time someone is observed performing a job task, and that task performance is below standard, that he/she be given a clear Development Goal (or multiple goals) of what the expected better performance is to be. With each of those goals, it is then necessary to identify the specific Action Items that will take place that will lead this person to better job performance of the specific job task.

Keep in mind, if you really want to achieve lasting change, a person can only master a limited number of changes at one time. While performance may go up for a short period, it may only be caused by an intense focus on something, which, unless the underlying skill, knowledge, or behavior is elevated, will return to the lower level of performance once the focus shifts to something else. That's the payoff for managing improvement coaching using this crossover chain. If we know what contributes to the company's success, then we will invest the time to truly enhance the performance level of the people working towards the supporting tasks. A little effort will go a long way towards contributing measurable, sustainable results.

Goal Setting

A quick word on goal setting. As usual, there are volumes of great material out there on the topic of creating and managing goals. I'll refer you to those, but I do want to mention in summary how you must approach goal setting. The underlying message is that **goals must be clear**. To help ensure their clarity, some cleaver person came up with the SMART acrostic for the attributes of a good goals statement. You may find this helpful as you work on writing goals statements.

Writing SMART Performance Goals

➢ Specific (what is the expected performance)

➢ Measureable (how we will know the goal was achieved)

➢ Attainable (work against a performance standard)

➢ Realistic (a level at which this person really can work)

➢ Time Sensitive (set a deadline and stick to it!)

Performance & Accountability Reviews and Compensation

While this is not a book on management principles, techniques, and practices, if we're going to optimize employee job performance, individually and collectively, we must consider the role of management intervention in job performance. A healthy environment will have in it reward systems and punishment systems. It's all well and good to focus on how people respond in a positive direction to positive reinforcement, which should be the primary stimulus, but there are times when individuals and groups need to have a good prodding in order to get the results the business is after. With that in mind, let's discuss the two types of reviews: Performance Reviews and Accountability Reviews.

Employee Job Performance Reviews

A Performance Review consists of a discussion between a manager and an employee during which the manager explains how he or she has <u>observed</u> the employee performing a job task, and now the manager is trying help that person move his/her performance to a higher level. Even acceptable levels of performance can be moved higher, most of the time. The discussion should follow this basic flow:

1. a clear statement as to the success criteria for the task, based on objective measurement whenever possible;
2. statement as to how the individual's performance compares to the standard (can be accuracy of execution or level of output);
3. review the skills, knowledge, or behaviors that result in successful task execution;
4. identify the gap between the required s,k,b level and that of the individual;
5. agree on an action plan to close the gap;
6. schedule a follow-up discussion.

It's very important to focus on only one, or perhaps two job tasks at a time when trying to affect performance. When the target is to affect a mastery level of an enabling skill, knowledge, or behavior element, then the person can get better at that one thing, and he/she will "own" it forever. When we fill the sky full of lead, and give someone ten things to get better at, then he/she will only improve for a short time at best, due to the increase in focus from the manager on those areas, but when the focus changes and moves to something else, then the behavior will return to the old level because the underlying enablers have not changed.

If it's important to focus on only one or two items to facilitate lasting change, then it follows naturally that one must have these "performance reviews" frequently or else change will take forever. That's why there are two types of reviews. Performance reviews should take place on a regular basis. In fact, they should be constant. Think of these as "coaching sessions." The manager should be constantly coaching the employee on how to do better at the execution of the job tasks. That means that these shouldn't be extensive discussions, but they should be focused and they should be constant.

A best practice for performance reviews is to have a regularly scheduled time with each employee to discuss where they are with mastery of whatever job task you have them currently focused on improving. A more senior employee will need fewer coaching sessions, so probably once per month will be sufficient. Rookie employees may need these discussions weekly. Keep in mind, these are not extensive discussions, so they can be handled efficiently by a manager. Also keep in mind that increasing the employee performance level should be a primary concern for any manager, and this approach will lead to lasting results.

People rise or fall to the expectations of others

An interesting phenomena of human behavior is how people respond to the expectations of others. While there are exceptions to every rule, a large percentage of people are influenced in their behavior by the perception others have as to how well or poorly they will perform. When someone has confidence in a person, that person tends to do better than they would have with a neutral coach. Unfortunately, the opposite is also true: when someone gives an impression of a lack of confidence in someone else's ability to perform a job, then that person tends to perform at lower levels than he/she would have with a neutral coach.

Now, lest you think I'm advocating the "cheerleader" approach to management, let me temper these observations with a word of grounding in reality. Confidence is only contagious when the recipient has reason to also become confident. If the coach is either always saying "you can do it" then the words become empty after awhile, and lose their effect, but if the words are not also accompanied with some prior or just-in-time training, then the recipient will lack the evidence that he/she has reason to expect success, and will not rise to the higher expectations. Conversely, if someone has been trained to a certain level, he/

she tends to be a bit immune to the negative draw of lower expectations. This person adopts a variation of the "I'll show them" mentality. However, even the most confident person can begin to succumb to self-doubt when those around him/her continue in their fear of uncertain results. Bottom line: be a confidence boosting coach through task enablement. Developing skills is only one part of top performance, your setting higher expectations, with sincere and fact based encouragements to expect success, is also a necessary component.

Employee Job Accountability Reviews

But Performance Reviews are only one part of the review ingredient to the Workforce Optimization recipe. The other part is the Accountability Review. Performance Reviews are intended to coach an employee forward by focusing on the <u>execution</u> of specific job tasks and the enabling skills, knowledge, and behaviors. To properly manage employee job performance, there needs to also be a formal accountability mechanism in place to regularly measure and document how each person is performing, particularly with regard to <u>output</u> quality and quantity, when compared to the job's standards. These are often accompanied with a discussion of compensation adjustments, which is a logical connection. Performance Reviews, on the other hand, should not be tied to an Accountability Review or a compensation adjustment, but we'll get to that in a few pages.

While it's apparent that in order to hold someone accountable for job performance the organization needs to know what the acceptable performance level is for each job, I want to highlight that foundational need so that you can see in a moment how P.E.R.F.O.R.M. supports employee reviews by also documenting job performance information. So, hold that thought . . .

Before we leave the subject of employee reviews, take a minute to reflect on how and when reviews should occur in connection with discussions about compensation. Consider the different situations in which you may find yourself as a manager of people.

It's in the realm of Job Accountability Reviews that a management principle comes into play, which, if this factor is missing, can undermine the impact of these two types of performance reviews: **A little professional distance between a manager and a subordinate is a good and useful thing**. While I really like the image created by calling managers "coaches," being an employee's "pal" without being his/her "boss" corrupts the dynamic that is essential to stimulate behavior change when it's needed. A little professional distance goes a long way to keep the unspoken carrot and stick forces BOTH available to a manager. Once an employee feels that his/her boss is his/her "friend" it becomes very hard for that boss to enforce discipline. Both the manager and the employee need to honor this "space," while at the same time being open to developing a friendship. There's nothing wrong with being friends, but there should always be the understanding that at times everyone needs a little push, and the company has created management layers in order to have a method to apply a push when and where it's needed.

As we begin, keep in mind, when I use the term "great raise" or "marginal raise" I'm using it from the receiver's point of view. It really doesn't matter in these situations what the giver thinks of the quantity of the raise, it's the resulting impact in the life of the receiver that we're looking at. We need to decide if different ways to manage reviews will achieve the results we're after. Oh, let's agree on the results we're after – improved job performance.

Oh, and we need to agree on a concession before we go further too. Anytime you give someone a raise you will see a bump in job performance, and anytime you deny someone a raise (remember, we're looking at the perspective of the receiver not the giver) you will see a dip in job performance. The result we're trying to analyze in the regard to impact of a salary review at the same time as a performance review is **sustained** job performance – does it go up or down for a **sustained** period of time?

Scenario One: Perfect or Acceptable Performer, Good Raise. Here we see someone who is a recognized performance leader in the company. He/She already believes himself/herself to be valuable to the company. As they come in the door to your office they're expecting a raise. A good raise. All you can do is either meet that expectation by awarding a good raise, or else offend them with a marginal raise. We all can guess the effect of a marginal raise, but what about the effect of a good raise?

Awarding a good raise is really only meeting what they expected to happen. You could get a good bump in performance if you award a great raise, but either way, good or great raise, they're going to enter your office thinking they're performing up to standard (or better) and they're going to leave your office thinking they're performing up to standard (or better.) You will not have impacted their perception of their job performance to such an extent that you will alter their behavior. The only way to do this is to blast their performance while giving a good raise, which will send a mixed signal, and you'll still only temporary performance change, only this time it will be no change or a dip!

Scenario Two: Perfect or Acceptable Performer, Marginal Raise. A bit more tenuous ground here! Now we're in a situation where we have good performance, but for whatever reason, you can only award a marginal raise. Perhaps there's a company-wide moratorium, or perhaps this person is at or near the salary cap for the position. For whatever reason, the raise is marginal.

So, he or she sits through the discussion about how their job performance is good, all the while waiting to find out what the reward is. Does this cause them to think "I need to do a better job"? No. I causes them to think "ok, I can check that off as ok, now for the good part!" It's the same mindset as in scenario one, only, because there is no "good part" coming, the results are disastrous.

Time for the salary part of the discussion. As they learn that they're in fact not getting the raise they believe they're entitled to (which, by the way, is the same mindset the OK Performer will have in this situation, even though he/she really is only entitled to a marginal raise!) as the reality sinks in, their attitude will begin to tank, and they'll leave your office on a track for decreased job performance.

Now I'll put on an optimistic hat and suggest that you may recover this person over time. If he/she was a good performer in the past, he/she probably has the right attitude, and will self-recover over time. However, you better hope, or make sure, that this person doesn't encounter someone in the next two scenarios while he/she is in this tenuous middle ground!

Scenario Three: Marginal or Lousy Performer, Marginal Raise It's hard to say which scenario is the worst, scenario two or this one. In scenario two you negatively impact job performance, and possibly alienate a good performer. In this scenario you reward bad behavior!

Let's look at the employee's mindset coming into the "review" … He/She may know that his/her job performance is sub par, but most people either are blind to this or else they justify it into submission. I've never had an employee, in a salary review setting, tell me that his/her job performance is below standard. If they even get close, what follows is a litany of reasons why it's someone or something else's fault. I never enjoy those conversations. I think it's safe to assume they will either enter your office in blissful ignorance, expecting a good raise, or else they'll enter in defense mode. Both lead to the same mindset as they leave your office two bloody hours later.

So during your "review" discussion, this person learns, or is forced to admit, that his/her job performance is unacceptable. You may even have a good discussion about how to improve it. HOWEVER, they're still sitting there waiting for the "good part," which they're already suspecting will actually be the "bad part."

Time for the salary part of the discussion. Bad news – marginal raise. That's probably the best thing you can do with a lousy or even marginal performer. The thing with this is that you've reinforced the idea that someone can perform at minimum acceptable levels or below, and they still get a bump. What worries me the most about this scenario is the cancer it will spread. Let's face it, while people may not talk about the specific money they make or receive in their annual "review," they do talk in terms that let someone else get the general idea of how things went, up or down. Even if they went down, people aren't going to admit that in public, in front of their peers. The only time this happens is when two or more people create a cancer ward.

Had we built an audit trail of regular job performance observation coaching sessions having some effect throughout the past year, then we could better justify a positive compensation adjustment at year end, even though overall performance still needs to improve. But, if we're going to have the two conversations at the same time, forget it.

Scenario Four: Marginal or Lousy Performer, No Raise. This is a no-win situation. You are just simply not going to get better performance out of this person. The best you can hope for is to "scare them into better performance," but I'd argue that this is temporary at best. If you'd had a healthy performance coaching session separate from a compensation discussion, then maybe you'd have an impact. When coupled with the comp discussion, no chance. Well, ok, slim chance. That's as far as I'll go.

In all four scenarios I can build a pretty good case that you won't get the results you're after if you tie a performance discussion together with a compensation discussion. The only compromise I'm willing to agree to is to couple the accountability review with the compensation discussion. I can see where they reflect on one another, so I can see, for efficiency's sake, why you'd put them together. But NEVER with a performance review. It undermines the impact you're after!

If, instead, you always discuss how to improve job performance on an ongoing basis **with everyone**, not just top or bottom performers, then you stand a better chance of getting job performance to improve. The receiver of the coaching will be in a different mindset. When money comes into a discussion, the focus always shifts. It's human nature, and it's unavoidable. If you want to see sustained, improved job performance, you need to have an environment that focuses on performance observation and coaching, with periodic accountability and compensation discussions.

I **don't** think companies continue to have compensation reviews along with accountability reviews along with performance improvement coaching all at the same time because they're too stupid to realize this just doesn't achieve the results they're after. I think it's because it's an administrative nightmare in most companies to discuss job performance improvement, and this cause companies to continue to lump all of this together into one Annual Review (or, at best, a Quarterly Review of performance, and then one Annual Review where all three are discussed).

If we only had an easier way to have regular performance coaching sessions, and then if only we could easily compile that information to have handy when it came time to discuss compensation adjustments …   I'm glad you asked!

This first element of making it easier to gauge and discuss an employee's performance comes is clearly communicating job expectations. To that end, P.E.R.F.O.R.M. has a placeholder in the Jobs definition form that lets you record the accountability factors for a particular job.

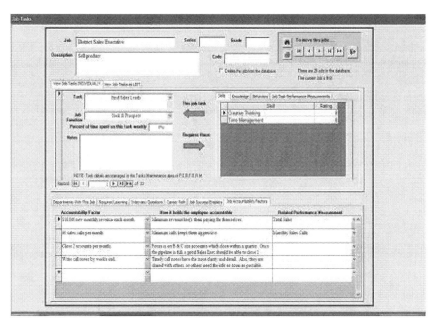

P.E.R.F.O.R.M. Screen– Job Tasks

When you choose a specific job, and then click on the tab labeled "Job Accountability Factors" in the bottom portion of the form, you can create a list of expectations for the chosen job. To identify a new factor for a particular job, you need only choose it from a pick-list in the first (far left) column. If you want to specify a new accountability factor that has never been used for any other job, it will not be in the pick-list, so you will need to type it in the blank space. After that, it will show up in the list for future use. Each factor also has a column that lets you explain how and/or why it's an accountability factor for the specific job, and then, and probably the most important part, you identify the performance measurement that will be used to find out how well an employee doing this job is doing against the accountability factor. "Don't expect what you don't inspect, and you can inspect what you don't detect." Well, that last part wasn't as clever as I had hoped it would be, but I think you grasp my intent.

Also remember that each job is defined by the specific tasks performed by someone employed to do the job. This is the list in the middle of the screen.

We'll use each of these two areas on the Job Tasks form in order to conduct a "review" of an employee.

Accountability Reviews in P.E.R.F.O.R.M.

When you first click on the Accountability Review button on the Main Menu, you are asked to identify the person for you'd like to see existing Accountability Reviews and/or create a new Accountability Review.

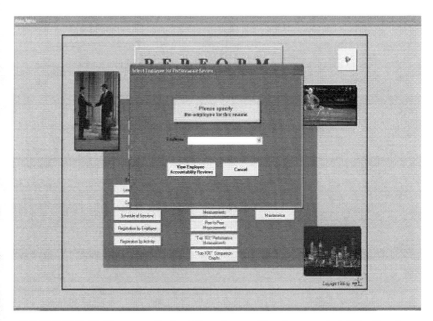

P.E.R.F.O.R.M. Screen– Select Employee For Accountability Review

Once you identify the person for the Accountability Review, P.E.R.F.O.R.M. opens the Accountability Review form. You will first see any existing review forms the person you picked. The display at the top will tell you how many total Accountability Reviews there are for the person you chose, and the number of the one you are currently viewing.

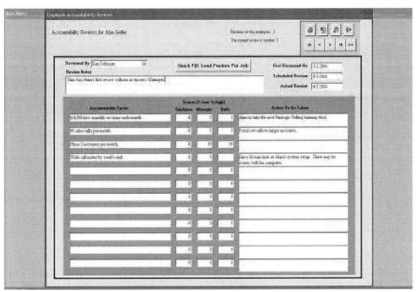

P.E.R.F.O.R.M. Screen– Accountability Review

Here is an explanation of the fields, buttons, and tabs on this form:

Item Name	What It's For
Title with reviewed person's name	When you choose Accountability Review form the Main Menu, you are prompted to identify who you are working with. All existing reviews for that person are brought up, and his/her name appears in the title. The number of total reviews for that person, and the number of the review you are on, appears to the right in the title area. Any new reviews will automatically be associated with the same person.

Required Learning | Interview Questions | Career Path | Job Success Enablers | Job Accountability Factors | Job Task Performance Measurements
Skills | Knowledge | Behaviors

Quick Fill: Load Factors For Job button	Explained in detail in the following section, but this lets you jump-start your review by filling in the default factors from the job definition this person holds.
Accountability Factor field	These are free-from text fields that can be whatever element you are entering a grade for. You can quick fill the list (using the button), and then edit those entries, or you can just start typing.
Score columns	A good review will capture both the manager's and the employee's scoring opinion for each factor, and then the agreed to score.
Scheduled and Actual Review fields	These are for subsequent discussions related to these factors and scores, not the initial review.
Print Button	This is the typical print button, but for Accountability Reviews only, the form that prints has a **signature line** for both the employee and the manager. Signed reviews make nice audit trails . . .
Grant S,K,&B's button	In this form, this button credits the employee with all of the s,k,&b for all of the job tasks done by someone in this job. THIS IS A VERY POWERFUL thing to do, but is appropriate for someone who has mastered his/her job.

Action To Be Taken field	I'm not even sure why I'm including this in the grid it seems so obvious, but, this is where you document what both parties are going to do to address the item. This is different than a development plan against a deficiency in being able to do a task. We'll talk about that in a minute when we get to Performance Reviews.

When you want to create a new Accountability Review, you click on the New Record button in the menu area at the top right, and P.E.R.F.O.R.M. will move to a blank form, but will automatically associate it with the person you chose when you opened the Accountability Review area. To start entering your information into the form, you can start typing the factors you are going to rank into the column on the left. However, always vigilant for productivity, P.E.R.F.O.R.M. will let you jumpstart your factors list by using the Quick Fill button, in this case it is "Quick Fill: Load Factors For Job" to populate the factors column with those factors that were identified back on the Job Tasks form for whatever is the current job of the person this review is for. You can then edit or remove an auto-populated entry, and then add others if you need them.

If you choose to print this Accountability Review form, P.E.R.F.O.R.M. will print a paper with signature spaces for both the reviewer and the employee. My suggestion is that this will help compile a nice audit trail should any future question arise as to an employee's Accountability Review history.

Oh! You'll see in just a minute (if you keep reading) how regular coaching sessions can be documented and printed, and make a great way to review and prepare for one of these Accountability Reviews.

Required Learning | Interview Questions | Career Path | Job Success Enablers | Job Accountability Factors | Skills | Knowledge | Behaviors | Job Task Performance Measurements

But that's only one part of the review process … If we want job performance to improve, we need to have an easy way to discuss job performance with an employee!! Enter the Performance Review form!

Required Learning | Interview Questions | Career Path | Job Success Enablers | Job Accountability Factors | Skills | Knowledge | Behaviors | Job Task Performance Measurements

CROSSING OVER

Performance Reviews Revisited (and expanded!)

We've already discussed this a few pages back, but we're coming back to it and taking it a little further, now that we've better understood Accountability Reviews. Remember to think of these as "coaching sessions" because, as we discussed in the previous part of this section, that's what should be the spirit of a Performance Review. It's the manager coming alongside an employee to help him/her move his/her job performance higher. Remember, these are NOT accountability reviews, which make sure the employee is performing up to the job standards or better. The Performance Review is an ongoing dialog between an employee and his/her boss about how skills, knowledge, and/or behaviors can be changed, and thusly bring about higher performance levels.

I've already mentioned in the previous section about how Performance Reviews should focus on one or two things at a time. This lets the employee AND the manager focus. Once the new skill or knowledge is acquired, it will remain, and then the next thing can be tackled.

What I'd like to look at now, is the whole motivation on the part of the Manager to actually use this approach to improving performance. I have seen too many times a Manager who wants to see job output increase take the wrong approach, and, in the end, not only do things not get better, they get much worse. Consider the scene in the board room . . .

Bob runs the manufacturing department of the company. In the weekly management meeting, someone points out that the output of widgets per person is down this week. Everyone looks at Bob. Now Bob has two choices, he can either go back to the floor and tweak and fine tune the processes and the people's skills and knowledge, or he can go back to the floor and apply management pressure to coerce higher output. Let's see … Option one would take a lot of time, money, and effort, especially from Bob. Option two would require finding the right people to threaten and push, with a slight risk of elevated blood pressure on Bob's part. Option two gets immediate results. Hmmm. Bob chooses option two!

So Bob leaves the boardroom and makes his way to the production floor, all the while figuring out his strategy. Now Bob's not a bad guy, he's just under pressure to get results. It's the same results we've been talking about all along, financial results, it's just that there are two paths to go down to achieve those results. Too often we choose the path of least time to see results. Let's look at the results Bob achieves . . .

He hits the production floor revved up are ready to have a management intervention. He calls the group together, explains the pressure from "the top" that he just got in the board room, and vows to take drastic measures if things don't get better. Soon! With a good scowl around the collection of nervous and tensioned faces, he turns and goes back to his office. As the crown disperses, amid comments as of "What's up with Bob today?" they return to the production floor knowing that if things don't get better, something's going to get worse.

Oh, a quick qualifier – this is one of the first times Bob has taken this approach.

Now what would you do if you were one of those employees? I know what I'd do, because I've been there, and I know what I did. I used to load trucks for a warehouse operation, and when I heard the "get busier or else" address to the group, I got busier. Sure enough, that's what Bob's team did too. End result, productivity went up. The next week in the board room, productivity reports showed Bob's team up by 7%! There are "high-fives" around the board room table, Bob gets a "well done" from the COO, and everyone leaves in a good mood this week.

But why did productivity go up? And how long will it last?

I think we all know what happens to the productivity level in Bob's shop after a little time goes by. The level goes back down, and maybe lower, because NOTHING changed. The only thing that changed was a short-term **external** motivator, that will have a temporary effect on behavior, in this case, productivity levels. But because the people doing the job are human and not robots, the "engagement" element (there's more on "Employee Engagement" coming in a few chapters …) is damaged due to what will be perceived as improper treatment. Like it or not, agree with it or not, it's the way people respond. Now Bob will have to resort to bigger and bigger "hammers" to get the short-term boosts.

The reality of this approach though, is that **there will be short-term gain**. Sometimes that's all that matters. I told you I intended to talk candidly throughout this recipe book, and here's one of those "reality check" moments. It may be that it makes more sense, from a Return On Investment perspective, to use these "management interventions" to stimulate periodic spikes in performance. While I don't agree with this conclusion, it is one that we should all anticipate as a possibility.

I think you could probably guess at what I do advocate. Regular, ongoing, coaching on what a boss is observing as he or she watches an employee do his or her job. Once the proper steps in a process are identified (though classic business-side-of-the-house efforts) and the way to do the tasks are identified (through the same methods), then the employees need to be trained in how to do the job tasks (the tip of the pyramid of learning) and then constantly coached on how they are applying what they learned. Better, **long-term results** come from continual coaching.

Now, when I use the term "performance coaching" and "Performance Reviews," what I really mean is that someone has literally watched someone perform a job task (someone who knows the proper way to do the task, maybe while using a tip sheet) while looking for specific aspects of the proper way to do the task, and then the observer gives the performer specific comments on what worked correctly, what worked incorrectly, and why both either succeeded or failed. Remember, one or two things at a time. By pointing out specific things for the performer to work on, tips to get better, the performer can focus on those, and will achieve sustainable performance improvement.

Performance Reviews and P.E.R.F.O.R.M.

There is a module in P.E.R.F.O.R.M. that lets you record observations of an employee doing a job task. Keep in mind, that elsewhere we defined jobs in the company, and we also broke down those jobs into the tasks people in those jobs perform. Also, remember that P.E.R.F.O.R.M. lets us set up a Learning Experiences catalog of all the things the company has at its disposal to teach people how to do the job tasks, and remember that when we defined the Learning Experience we identified the Learning Outcomes in terms of job tasks enabled by the Learning Experience. Well check out how these pieces come together in P.E.R.F.O.R.M. . . .

Piece number one: the actual Performance Review form.

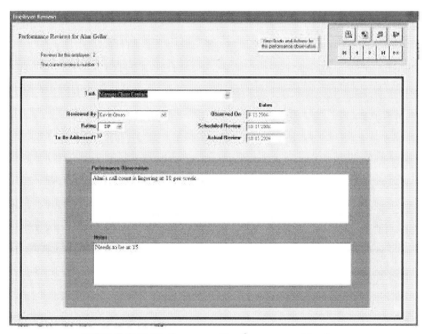

P.E.R.F.O.R.M. Screen– Performance Review

The very first thing that you identify with a Performance Review is who its for, obviously, but then you pick the single task you have observed. It forces you to focus! Once you pick the person and the task, you fill out the necessary housekeeping fields for who you are (Reviewed By), the date of the observation, and when it was discussed.

P.E.R.F.O.R.M. also lets you flag two important distinctions about every observation: was this a Best Practice (something done well) or a Developing Practice (something that needs work) by using the Rating field. Sometimes we document Best Practices for someone doing a job task. While this has a nice warm-and-fuzzy effect on the person being documented as mastering the job task (hence identifying it as a "Best Practice") and we all know how much HR people live for warm-and-fuzzy moments, it really is for a large, more useful purpose, not that pats on the back aren't useful. In another area of P.E.R.F.O.R.M. you are able to review all of these Best Practice records, tied to specific Performance Measurements you're trying to boost!! If someone needs to bring up their performance in a specific area, as indicated by a low number in the corresponding performance measurement that helps the company track results, then he or she can open the Best Practices area of P.E.R.F.O.R.M. and select that performance measurement, and all of the Best Practices that are related to how people are doing the job tasks that were documented in the Jobs form as affecting that performance measurement are brought up for the person to read and learn from. They find out how someone is doing the job tasks well, and may even reach out to that person for some insight. It makes the whole organization a learning and mentoring organization!

But I digress … back to the Performance Review, and let's explore what happens if this person gets a "developing practice" rating for his or her performance of the job task being observed.

The other element that P.E.R.F.O.R.M. lets you flag is, if it's a developing practice, do you want to address it, or just have it documented. No matter how this flag is set, you'll still record your observation notes in the field for Performance Observation (what you saw) and the Notes field (what you think about what you saw.) These two fields make up the heart of the performance review.

Now, if you want to address the developing practice through some learning experience, then you'd checkmark the "To Be Addressed?" flag, and click on the "View Goals and Actions" button towards the top right of the form. That will open up a second level of detail for this Performance Review which will let you create an action plan for how you will address the performance deficiency you observed.

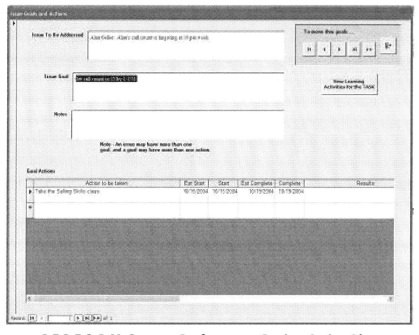

P.E.R.F.O.R.M. Screen– Performance Review Action Plan

P.E.R.F.O.R.M. carries the entry from the previous form over and displays it on the Action Plan form, just so you won't forget what you're addressing, and now you can specify the goal for the improvement, and also set specific action steps, with specific dates of accountability. If we're going to address the problem, let's have a clear plan of attack!

Required Learning   Interview Questions   Career Path   Job Success Enablers   Skills   Job Accountability Factors   Knowledge   Behaviors   Job Task Performance Measurements

Just in case you're not sure what you have at your disposal to apply in your quest to help this person get better, the Action Plan form has a button that lets you open the Learning Experiences catalog and view entries where the job task being addressed is part of the learning outcomes **AND**, because when we defined the job tasks we also defined the skills, knowledge, and behaviors needed to perform is, and when we defined the Learning Experience we also cataloged the skills, knowledge, and behaviors it taught, this button also pulls in any Learning Experience that addresses ANY of the skills, knowledge, or behaviors needed for the job task being addressed, even if it's not a specific learning outcome!

P.E.R.F.O.R.M. Screen– Learning Activities Filtered for Performance Review

Just because you came into the catalog from a Performance Observation Action Plan form doesn't mean you will always only need to look at related learning experiences. P.E.R.F.O.R.M. tries to help you decide on a possible intervention, but you may also want to look at other items for possible use. If you click on the "Show All Learning Activities" button at the bottom right of the form, P.E.R.F.O.R.M. will remove the filters used

Required Learning | Interview Questions | Career Path | Job Success Enablers | Job Accountability Factors | Job Task Performance Measurements

Skills | Knowledge | Behaviors

from the Action Plan form, and you'll be able to look at all of the items in the catalog for possible use to address the performance deficiency.

Of course, at the end of all your data entry, you can print the Performance Review form if you want to use the paper for your discussion with the employee, or if you need them to sign the form for your formal audit trail records. I don't believe there is much need for signed coaching reviews, but there should be signed Accountability Reviews. You decide for yourself, P.E.R.F.O.R.M. will support you either way.

Show Me The Money!

I live by what I advocate (show the tie to the money,) so let me give you some measurements to back up what I'm suggesting.

When I measured this approach at 24 companies in the US, Latin America, and Europe, and compared those with traditional annual review strategies to those with both Performance Reviews and Accountability Reviews ("Balanced Review Approach"), here were the results:

	3 Year Avg Growth Rate	
	Annual Review Approach	Balanced Review Approach
Small	12%	24%
Medium	24%	32%
Large	18%	27%

What the data told me is that the "balanced review approach" yielded a **100%** improvement in small companies (25-100 employees); a **33%** improvement in medium sized companies (101 – 2,500 employees); and a **50%** improvement in large sized companies (more than 2,500.) There was marked improvement in how well and fast employees performed their jobs, and the results in company growth followed.

FYI - These measurements are company revenue results. The companies chosen for this analysis were all 3-10 years in existence, in an effort to isolate "start-up" and "growing stagnant" elements from skewing the study measurements. I used 8 small, 8 medium, and 8 large companies, and, for each size, measured 4 with a traditional approach and 4 with a balanced approach. The largest workforce I've helped to implement a balanced review approach has about 10,000 employees.

Whose Job Is It Anyway?

Another of the key elements to any company's success in training and development is a healthy realization as to who is responsible for employee performance. So the next question we need to answer is "whose job is it anyway?" The answer is, of course, it's everyone's job. We are all in this together, so we may as well all work towards the common good. When employees perform to their maximum potential, they gain, it reflects well on the direct manager, so he or she gains, and the company gains by having higher performance.

There's a catch to this, though. There are three roles, and if any of the three don't contribute their part, then the whole program breaks down. So let's take a moment to discuss the responsibilities of these three roles.

Role One: The Company

It is the responsibility of the company to foster the proper atmosphere, or environment, for optimum performance. This includes, but is not limited to, fair compensation plans for every employee. Here's where the old adage still applies: "the workman is worth his wages." Well, now we may be inclined to say worth his or her wages, but the idea is still the same. But there's more to this responsibility than just pay. A fair compensation plan includes things like proper performance reviews, healthy working conditions, and rewards that matter to the employees, not just the management team.

Think back to our discussion on the attitude ingredient of our Workforce Optimization recipe. The company begins to define the environment which either fosters or undermines "fairness." You will do one or the other, whether you actively intend to or not! The Manager role, the role we'll look at next, takes what the company sets in motion and either prospers the healthy environment or squelches it.

Just in case you think I'm an Ivory Tower HR idealist, I'll go on record as saying that the first and foremost responsibility of the company is to make sure it remains healthy. That means profitable and competitive. Let me phrase it in the form of a question. Who would want to work at a company that lavishes rewards on its employees while it slowly loses market share? How about while it slowly goes out of business because there isn't enough profit to reinvest in new ideas?

While I'd argue that the company who fulfills its obligation to its employees will never have to worry about this, I want to be accurate and state that the reason a company has a Management Team is to hold the employees accountable for doing living up to their responsibility in the effort. The company has a two-fold responsibility that creates a balancing act: satisfaction of customers and satisfaction of employees.

Role Two: The Management Team

The primary responsibility of the management team is to fairly assess employee job performance, provide coaching to address deficiencies, and reward the growth of performers, and punish those who refuse to perform (notice I <u>didn't</u> say "punish those who **can't** perform!) Now the company will look to these same managers to also know the best and most efficient ways to accomplish whatever the area over which they manage is expected to contribute. If a person manages the widget production area, then the company expects that person to not only know how to manage the people who do the job, but also to know the best way to produce widgets. Since we're trying to understand Workforce Optimization, let's confine our discussion to the people element of management. That's enough!

It's funny how you can get more with less. What do I mean? Let me tell you about a recent experience I had in the Middle East. I was traveling on behalf of a world-wide company to their Middle East Regional Headquarters in Beirut, Lebanon. Don't believe all you hear and read – I liked the place. Anyway, two years prior I had visited the same city for a training event with the same group, only at that time they had 124 people in this particular department. The department was also generating about $400,000 per year in annual sales. The Region's Director instituted a policy of zero tolerance for non-performers. For years the company had established performance standards, let's say 100 widgets per week per person, but tolerated people who only made the mark to 60%. That was the start of the trouble. It created an atmosphere of "we can't go higher." The new zero tolerance policy meant that anyone not performing up to standard was put on notice, and then began a six month period of consistent coaching. At the six-month mark, if performance was still below standard, the determination was made as to whether it was an attitude issue or an ability issue. If it was an ability issue, and there was another job fit for the individual within the company, the employee was repositioned. If it was an attitude issue, and even after 6 months of focused coaching they still would not come around, then the company honored their unspoken request to no longer be employed there. The persistent non-performers had to be let go.

In the end, some employees were moved, some were removed. It may sound harsh, but I believe it is the absolute best environment a manager can create. It is the essence of fairness. In fact, to keep non-performers is not "fair." Of course the standards were checked and rechecked, and it was determined that there were a significant number of those who were at or above the mark, so all was established as accurate. When I returned two years later, there were 88 people in the department, but their annual sales had soared to $1.6 million! The really exciting part was to hear comment after comment from the workforce as to their feeling far better about their job now then they did in the "old days." They loved an atmosphere that sets the pace and then, for those who want to, helps people achieve it. Those who didn't want to perform at the team's set expectations were removed from the team, and those who were left liked it better!

This real world example illustrates what we all know to be true: winners like to be challenged. The successful company is the one that identifies or creates winners, and then challenges them to win. When mediocrity is tolerated, everyone lowers his/her threshold of challenge.

It's the responsibility of the management team to create and foster an atmosphere of fairness (let the results come, regardless of the perception of good or bad) but not as a surprise, and an atmosphere of challenge. Continue to set the goal higher and watch the workforce scale the mountain.

By the way – a few of the employees who were let go actually called their old Manager and thanked him! They told him they were truly excited about their new job and they regretted putting him, the old company, and themselves through the hardship of staying somewhere where they just weren't motivated. The voice of the manager in stimulating employee performance is a critical factor in reinforcing the work done in the Training and Development area of the company. As the job identifies areas of development need, creating relevance for learning, the Training group moves one or more learning experiences into the employee's world, but then the voice of the manager comes back into play. The person guiding the learning is able to use the job and manager's future expectations to create motivation and credence for the learning. As the manager coaches and holds accountable, he/she can refer the employee back to how the instructor demonstrated the essential elements of the task, and hence, the employee's behavior will improve. This dichotomy of voices, one doing initial explaining and one coaching as the new skills are further tested and mastered, is the best recipe for faster improvement. It doesn't have to take two, it just helps when there's two!!

Role Three: The Employee

Now let's not forget that the employee has some responsibilities in this ecosystem too! It is the responsibility of the employee to always do the tasks expected of him or her to the absolute of his or her ability. I like to think of the primary employee responsibility as being to bring a proper ATTITUDE. Of course they are also expected to bring job skills and knowledge, that goes without saying, but often that's the only element checked, while it is the attitude that sets everything in motion.

When I was a kid in the 60's, a cartoon called *Gulliver's Travels* made its debut. Interestingly enough, that was the first book I ever read cover to cover as a young adult in college, but that's beside the point here. Anyway, in *Gulliver's Travels*, the cartoon, there was a character named Glum. He can be summarized by his signature line "we'll never make it." Now you have to read that in a monotone, sort of downer type voice. Once you get it, you'll understand the mind of Glum. I think Glum was a disillusioned perfectionist, not that there's anything wrong with being a perfectionist. Good luck. But anyway, the reason I'm bringing him up here is to illustrate how one bad apple can spoil the whole bunch. Not that apples come in bunches. If someone is of the Glum personality type, my advice is find a new home for him or her. If you're that person, get help. You've probably fallen and you can't get up. I want to help, really. If you remain in the current state, you'll never find fulfillment. The employee MUST bring the right attitude to the job or else disaster always follows. Once again, it befalls the management role to make sure fairness prevails. When the wrong attitudes are allowed to persist, just like non-performance, it brings everyone down. You can't have an optimized workforce with Glum on the job. I know, for some reason we all like Glum. So help him/her. Tell them that the attitude has to go.

Just a note in case you thought I didn't mean what I implied in that last section. A key component to performance is attitude. It is just as important as skill and knowledge in determining the success or failure of a work group. When we recruit, hire, coach, promote, and fire, we need to strongly consider attitude and behaviors criteria. We ignore them at our own peril.

When all three of these roles are providing their responsibilities, the result is a fully engaged employee, and the workforce is ready to be optimized. When one or more of these roles withholds or falls short in its responsibilities, then problems are sure to follow. At a minimum, job performance is not at its fullest potential, and that's what we're trying achieve here.

Keep in mind, the group responsible for guiding the company as it concerns the "people factor" (the Human Resources Department, or the Organizational Development Department, or the Training Department, or the Workforce Optimization Department, whatever name your company uses …) will be working in concert with the people at each of these levels to make sure the right things are being done to optimize the overall workforce.

Workforce Optimization Support Tasks

Drives Training Development (vertical, left arrow pointing down)

Informs Training Design (vertical, right arrow pointing up)

Strategic (upper management)
- Set company vision
- Set company goals
- Review ROI & provide compensation

Workforce Optimization
- Analyze company level impact of job perf. improvement
- Design engagement practices that result in true ROI enhancement

Tactical (department managers)
- Oversee day to day operations
- Manage the workforce
- Perform tasks that support training efforts

- Analyze job impact of training
- Use historic data to identify high potential job candidates
- Create & execute management plan to support training events

Functional (front-line employees)
- Bring the right attitude
- Do the job tasks
- Give feedback

- Conduct training events that build ability
- Confirm post-class (formal event) mastery

Fully Engaged Employees Revisited (and expanded too!)

Way back in the early sections of this recipe book we talked about fully engaged employees. Let's get this ingredient back out of the pantry and onto the worktable, and look a little deeper into it. "Fully Engaged Employees" is a label for a key concept that you'll want to use over and over in your workplace, so we need to make sure we have a common understanding of what it means when we use it. Refer again to the diagram that follows, which you saw in the earlier section, and let's talk more about how Attitude and Ability must go together in an individual.

Fully Engaged Employee	• Master of his/her job • Sharing ideas • Improving processes

• Team Spirit
• Creative ideas
• Mentor role
	• Job specific skill and knowledge
	• Job performance feedback
	  ➤ measurements
	  ➤ reviews

• Work ethic • Co-operative Spirit	
Attitude	Ability

We've talked at length about how to best develop the ability side of the equation, and we'll spend a little more on that side of the equation, but for now, I want to touch on the attitude side. No matter how talented an individual is, none of that talent matters unless he or she is motivated to apply that talent to the job at hand.

Ideally we'll recruit and interview for attitude. You'll find more on that in the chapter that deals with Finding And Hiring The Best Possible People, but let's not loose sight of the contribution that the three roles need to bring to create and continue a proper attitude in the employees.

When employees feel like there is a disconnect between their efforts and the rewards and recognition programs, then disengagement follows. This is not always because the company or manager intended it. Most often it is because there are poorly designed reward and recognition programs. In all the years I've worked with and interacted with people, I've yet to meet anyone who has told me that they consider themselves OVER paid and under worked. In fact, it's always been quite the opposite. No matter how many people, from the outside looking in, would consider that Bob could in no way think he deserves the pay he receives, it's been my experience that Bob always thinks he deserves what he gets, and even should be getting more. I think it's a reality of the human condition. It's part of what keeps us sane (to the degree that any of us actually are.) I think there's a psychological mechanism that, no matter who we are or what we do, we look at it from our perspective, and we consider ourselves to be worth whatever it is we receive. No matter what we receive, we are convinced, in ourselves, that we should receive "more," whatever "more" means to each person.

Now I'm not saying this is a right perspective, or even a healthy perspective, in truth I think it quite unhealthy because it manifests in unhappiness more often than anything else. What it is, is the reality that we must confront if we are to try to achieve maximum employee "engagement." Regardless of why someone thinks they deserve "more" and regardless of, in a disconnected analytical way, they do or don't deserve "more," the employee thinks he deserves more, and this will drive his engagement or disconnection. Like it or not, it's where we must meet the person in the middle of the road.

I remember a job I had once where, because of personal connection, I became friends with my boss. We both were able to maintain a healthy work relationship in balance with our personal friendship, but we became close enough that he and I would have heart-to-heart conversations. On several occasions he vented his frustration about how his boss, who I also came to know well, treated him in a way that he felt was inequitable. It always amazed me at how the things he didn't like when he received them were some of the very things that I didn't like when he, in turn, did the same things with/to me! He certainly didn't mean to treat me inequitably, he just did. How is this possible? Because Bob always thinks he deserves "more." By the way, Bob is a name I use as a generality because I know more people named Bob than any other name. This guy's name wasn't Bob. I don't think I've ever worked for someone named Bob . . .

Anyway, let's see how this "I'm entitled to 'more'" mentality shows up in common business practices. Let's take a look at one of the most commonly adopted programs intended to foster good employee work attitudes – the Employee Of The Month program. Unless you have a rare work team on your hands, the Employee Of The Month results in one happy person, and the rest of the group alienated. Most people don't think someone else deserves whatever the reward is more than themselves. Also, keep in mind, the reward itself has to be substantial enough to cause people to want it. The days of people being proud to be the Employee Of The Month are gone. It takes more than pride to make the award a reward. So now you've invested in something that didn't get you the results you want.

I have seen some very successful Sales programs where the top 10% of the Sales force within categories (tenure in Sales or size of market, etc.) are publicized for their achievement, and the top Sales person is rewarded. Once again, I'm not naïve enough to think that those either not on the list or not at the top would actually be completely happy for the winner, but, if handled well, at least those on the list are happy, and, since the number one spot will probably change month to month, with a handful of people exchanging top place honors, enough tangible results can be gained by that group to make the program worthwhile.

So then how do we deal with the mentality of "I'm entitled to 'more'" without getting disgusted and firing people? Let them tell you what would motivate them! Let's agree right now that neither of us is smart enough to know what motivates everyone. We can come up with some generalities, which, if I couldn't offer some I wouldn't have the nerve to write this book, but we can't know for every person what it is that pushes his or her button. You may find that someone will bring their passion to the workforce if he/she gets to bring his/her child to a local day care. That means that your company will have to consider this as an option. Don't worry, I've been in the HR world long enough to know that there is a lot to consider when considering this, but let me still encourage you to look into it. I've seen it pay dividends in workforce motivation that I had never dreamed of. However, another employee, even if he/she has children, might not care at all if you have a daycare facility, so you're not going to get him/her to be passionate just because you have a new child care facility that Bob is all excited about. For this person maybe it's being able to have a flexible lunch time so that he/she can go to the gym at lunch three days per week.

Maybe you need to consider having a flexible work week schedule in general. I've seen four 10-hour days as a work week schedule make a huge difference in workplace passion if only because they get one day more to rest. With a staggering of staff so that some are out Monday, some Friday, and yes, some will even like being out another day of the week in order to take advantage of some outside activity during the week (maybe art classes on Tuesdays,) you'll find that coverage issues are lower than you think. The end result of this creative way of approaching "rewards" is passionate employees who feel that their employer is "working with them" to help them find balance in life, not just waving more money at them. After awhile, the majority of people are no longer motivated by financial rewards. It's ok to look for other motivators, and to use them. How do you know what they are for your employees? Ask them!

Well that was a bit off the beaten track of what we were discussing, fully engaged employees, but I wanted to flesh out a bit what an environment that fosters it might look like. It's all about finding ways to "involve" people who, let's face it, are "employees" not "owners" in the company. If they get the message, because it's true, that their company wants them to enjoy their job too, then they'll be more inclined to bring to the job the two elements you need: their passion and their creativity. Fully engaged employees do great things. Not just good things – great things! When an employee has passion, he/she cares about what he/she is doing. When you care, you make sure that your output is as good as you can possibly achieve. You no longer work against expectations or even goals, you work against your own potential. You always strive to reach higher because you're motivated within yourself, and that feeling of accomplishment is the ultimate measure of success. When an employee has creativity, even when he/she isn't the most gifted person from a creative or even intellectual perspective, he/she is still looking for ways to do things smarter, which leads to better, which leads to better results, from the company's point of view.

Now passion and creativity aren't the only necessary components to higher performance, one still needs to know how to apply those things in the workplace to achieve results. Just wanting to work smarter doesn't mean you can, you need to know how to analyze and make changes in order to work smarter.

What I'm trying to address here is the one missing component in most companies today: employees who **want to work**. When an employee is "fully engaged" he/she **wants** to work. These are the people who get up in the morning excited about going to work! Even the rush hour traffic can't dampen their spirits!

Before we move on, there is one Workforce Optimization factor that is critical to achieving an atmosphere that fosters fully engaged employees: job motivational fit. It will come up elsewhere in our little recipe book, but let me connect the dots here for just a minute. When someone is doing a job that "fits" their personality, the job itself rewards them. When we have a "people person" working in a customer service role, connecting with and satisfying a customer will, in itself, reward them.

Now keep in mind, the company has to have built into place the processes that let him/her truly take care of the customer, or else this has the exact opposite effect!

Conversely, when we take a "people person" and put him/her in front of a computer 8 hours a day, there's nothing more demotivating and that "fits" less with his/her personality. These people feel drained at the end of the day instead of energized.

To capture the spirit of "motivational fit" I'll use the words of a person I worked with to help him find his right job. Once he was in his new position for over a year (so this wasn't just the "honeymoon effect") he told me he had never been happier because he felt like he was "finally doing the job he was 'wired' for." In other words, it "fit" him, and that, in itself, regardless of the compensation it brought, was motivation. By the way, because he was fully engaged, he did great things, the company benefited, and he was rewarded. Everybody wins!!

The Unknown Variables Of Top Performance

We've spent a lot of time so far talking about how to work with the slippery yet knowable factors that effect employee job performance, we need to take some time to deal with the uncharted waters element of Workforce Optimization: unknown variables. These are the elements that affect job performance, either in a positive or negative way, that are not always specific to an individual, tend to be random and appear at first to be disconnected, but then, in hindsight, are discovered to have had a profound impact on the workforce or an individual.

For example, ever notice what happens when someone buys a new house? They work harder. Now I didn't intuitively know that would be the result, I realized it when I saw it happen over and over. That told me that if I wanted people to work harder, one simple way was to help them buy a new house. If we're hoping to obtain the highest degree of helping a company achieve high performance, the Workforce Optimization practitioner needs to be aware of, and to as much a degree as possible, be in control of, these unknown variables.

So what are these "unknown variables" that we're supposed to be in control of? I think it's easiest to explain using an example. Have you ever noticed what happens when a company moves to a new, better building? There are peaks and valleys in performance leading up to and during the move, but then there is a period of time during and just after the settling in period where job performance goes up. There is a definite impact on performance levels the better or worse the company planned the layout of the new facility, but the boost from employee moral usually outstrips the decrease from unfamiliar surroundings. You can almost feel the "buzz" in the air, and it's contagious, for awhile at least. The move to a new facility is an "unknown variable." There are others. The anxiety over Y2K a few years back took everyone into a productivity spiral. 9/11 in America is another example. A favorable jump of the company's stock might bring a productivity boost. Or maybe a productivity slump.

As we try to optimize job performance levels, then it becomes necessary to be aware of, and to as much a degree as possible, in control of, these unknown variables. Sounds familiar … didn't I just write that? Hmmm? Must be important.

If, when a favorable jump in the company's stock becomes known in the company, the job performance goes up, then we'll want to find ways to make sure the employees know when the stock goes up. Now that's a simple enough concept (I told you the concepts are easy in their individual focus!) but it is a bit difficult to track and manage unless you have a good job performance management tool (that's why I'm giving you P.E.R.F.O.R.M. with this book – you need the tools if you want to achieve the environment.)

A move to a new facility is a factor that will affect multiple people, but there are also factors that will affect only single individuals. Things like buying a new house or having a baby in the family will usually cause an increase in job performance due to a heightened appreciation for the job that provides for the new life enhancements. Or do they? One would have to look at the objective data to know for sure . . .

Over time, you can track the miscellaneous elements that you think will affect job performance up or down using that part of P.E.R.F.O.R.M. Then you'll take two approaches to see their effect:

1. Wait an appropriate amount of time after the element, and then check the various performance measurements you have, looking for changes in the performance levels.
2. As you see trends in performance levels during the course of normal monitoring of job performance measurements, then you open the area of P.E.R.F.O.R.M. used to track miscellaneous factors (available in multiple places in P.E.R.F.O.R.M.) and look for those that occurred in a close proximity to the performance peak or valley.

Once you know what affects individual and collective job performance, from an objective, data-driven foundation, you're ready to advise your company on how to use these factors to contribute to an optimized workforce.

P.E.R.F.O.R.M. has a section that lets you record any event that may turn out to affect job performance. This can be an event in the life of an individual, like buying a new house or having a baby, or an event that affects multiple people, like this shift structure change. As you see performance improvements or slips, you can review the Miscellaneous Factors area to see what events took place that may be related. In the case of our increased performance from the shift structure change, that lead to a review and adjustment to the work schedule for some, but not all, of our other positions in the company.

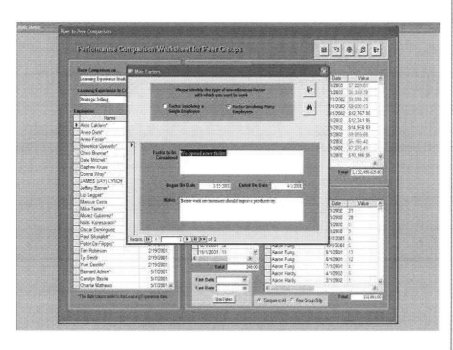

P.E.R.F.O.R.M. Screen– Miscellaneous Factors

Here is an explanation of the fields, buttons, and tabs on this form:

Item Name	What It's For
Multiple of Single radio button	The first thing you must specify is if the Miscellaneous Factor is for a single employee or many employees. If you choose a single employee, then you will have to identify the person you are working with. Once you do that, all of the existing Misc. Factors for that person will come up in the form. In the record bar at the bottom of the form, you'll see the total number of Misc. Factors for that person, and the number you are on. Any new items will automatically be related to that person. Many Employee Misc. Factors are not associated with any single person.
Factor To Be Considered field	This is a free-form text field that lets you store any event that might eventually be relevant in evaluating employee job performance, either as a group (Many Employees choice) or a single employee.

Item Name	What It's For
Begin and End Date fields	Knowing what happened will be of little value unless you record when the event started and ended. Then, later, as you look at changes in performance, you can find those Misc. Factors present before, during, or after the performance change.
Find button	I think you'll find this button VERY helpful in this form. There can be a lot of factors that accumulate over time, and this button will let you look through the full list of Misc. Factors related to Many Employees. I think the find list is what will help you best determine what factors might have been an influence on the performance you are evaluating.

Here's a lightening review of the mechanics of this handy little form. First, notice that a Miscellaneous Factor can be related to one person or many. If the company moved locations or opened a new product line, these factors will probably show up later as a factor that affected the job performance of many people. To help capture this anomaly so you can "factor" it into subsequent analysis, you would record it here as a factor involving many employees. It is important to look at the record indicator at the bottom of the form. Record: |◄| ◄| [1] ►|►|►*| of 2 It will tell you what number factor you are looking at in the overall list of all factors, whether it's all of the factors involving one person (in which case each person has his/her total number unto him/herself) or many. If you want to make a note of a new factor, remember to go to a new record, with a blank "Factor To Be Considered" field, before you start typing. If you type something new into the "Factor To Be Considered" field, and something is already in that field, you will be replacing your old information!

Anyway, you would capture these items over time, and then, when you are conducting performance analysis, as you see a trend, pattern, or anomaly, you can open the Miscellaneous Factors form to see if anything was going on around the time the phenomena occurred. If you see a spike in the job performance of a group of people, there's probably a common factor that caused it. Ideally you'd want to capture that factor, understand it, and, if possible, reproduce it to achieve the same bump.

Job Task Performance Measurements

Job Accountability Factors

Behaviors

Knowledge

Job Success Enablers

Skills

Career Path

Interview Questions

Required Learning

Chapter Seven:
The REALLY BIG Pay Off

- Performance Analysis

- Peer Comparison

- Finding and Hiring the Best Possible People

Performance Analysis

Now that we've covered substantial ground in discussing the pieces of Workforce Optimization and how they interrelate, it's time to introduce the big pay off: performance analysis. The real goal in all of this Workforce Optimization is to be able to more scientifically **identify** to the company those people who are top performers in their job, analyze how they got to be top performers, **help to find other candidates** who have the potential to become top performers, and then **enable and support** the company's and the individual's efforts to realize the employee's top performer potential. So the real key to sustaining and improving our Workforce Optimization approach is to focus **on top performers**, in a sense we are trying to "optimize" the time and effort it takes the company and its individual employees (the "workforce") to reach maximum job performance potential.

I'm being very careful NOT to say "to become top performers", because I don't believe in business "standards of performance." I believe you should always have a top 10% (or 20%, I'll be broader minded) that sets the pace for everyone else. The management team should always be investing in the top 10%-20% leaders to challenge them higher (but we also invest in the other 90%-80%, don't worry, I'm not just a cold-hearted capitalist!) but even those growth goals should be within a **HEALTHY** spirit of competition. No limits! The members of the top 10% should be dynamic, although there will always be some of the same names vying for the top spots, that's what champions do. Within this atmosphere of continual growth, some might call it the "pursuit of excellence," there will be those at the front of the pack, those at the middle of the pack, and those at the back of the pack. It's the way things are. The goal of Workforce Optimization is to help EVERYONE learn from the top 10%, and then to help each person, regardless of his/her position in the pack, to achieve to the maximum of his/her potential. But how can we help anyone get better if we don't know who those people are who have figured out how to succeed? That's why we need to look to our top performers!

So, if a company is going to get the most out of its investment in its people, then someone needs to understand and manage, and yes, I'll even say manipulate, some of the key elements that bring the greatest gain when considering employee potential:

The work experience with the highest payback.

The things top performers do that makes them top performers.

Training with the highest payback.

Which recruiting pond is better than another?

For what background to recruit.

Trends in an employee's job performance.

How one employee's job performance compares to his/her peers.

What an employee must do to prepare for career advancement.

If you recall in the previous chapter when we discussed how you know if your development was effective, I referred to Donald and James Kirkpatrick's 4 levels of evaluation. What I've seen through the years is that we do a pretty good job at levels one and two, post-class surveys and mastery tests, but we tend to assume there was a benefit at levels three and four, job impact and work impact. The real question is "did this intervention result in higher profits?" There is tremendous power in asking ourselves two little words: "**So What?**" (ok, two words and a question mark)

"We had a great class and people felt like they learned a lot."

"So what? Could they do their job better?"

"We gave a mastery test at the end and 95% could perform the tasks at or above the minimum acceptable level!"

"So what? Could they do it out at the job? Were they doing it that way one month later? One year later?" (Ouch! That's steeping on ROI toes!)

"Life is great, Mr. Smarty Pants. I checked and they're doing it that way even after a year!"

"So what? Did it make the output any better?" (now we're really getting at ROI!)

"I knew you'd ask that, so I checked, and yes, output is up, and so is quality!"

"Glad to hear it! How about revenue and profitability?" (as if level 3 wasn't good enough, now we're asking about level 4!)

"Ok, you've got me there. I wanted to check that because I knew you'd ask, (I read the Kirkpatricks' book after I read about it in your other chapter,) but I couldn't find anyway to check it."

"That's ok, we'll figure it out now! Together!"

Now there may be some intervening steps where payback is directly attributed,  but there should always be a clear path back to the profitability of the company. I think this is hard to do at first, but it becomes easier as you train yourself to think like the ROI Executives, and also if you have a tool (like P.E.R.F.O.R.M. that's included with this book.) Let's look at an example. We might consider that by the very nature of participating in a training class, an employee feels that the company is investing in him or her, and therefore he or she feels more valued, which leads to a boost in job performance levels. This is a wind-fall benefit that comes in addition to any heightened skill or knowledge level. The challenge I'd put to this reasoning is that, while I'm in agreement with the thought, it's not good enough. We should never train people **just because** it makes them feel more valued (even though that's one benefit.) There should be either another, greater ROI, or we should be able to trace that new "good feeling" to the boost in job performance, and that should be traced to the resulting higher output level, or maybe a reduced negative element. The "good feeling" job impact doesn't make me feel good about spending my training dollars on that particular course. Not only that, once you see the theory of Workforce Optimization to trace the trail back to the profit, then it is usually easy to figure out how the connection fits. If you can't find a fit, then don't continue the course.

Keep in mind that there are **two reasons why we need this job performance analysis** in our Workforce Optimization environment:

1. To check the level three and level four **impact of training events**;
2. To **identify top performers**, so we can see how they got that way, so we can use that insight to develop more top performers.

As you look at how P.E.R.F.O.R.M. supports the performance analysis needs, you'll see that it is both for those times when we're looking to see who is a top performer, because we truly don't know, and also to see if someone we are managing or thinking of is a top performer, or at least to understand what his/her performance level really is . . .

Peer comparison

The ROI topic leads directly to the next logical question (after "so what?") and this "How?" How can I determine if there was a payoff? The good news is that it's easy if you use P.E.R.F.O.R.M. and the better news is that it's included for free with the purchase of this book! Check the inside of the back cover for info. on how to get your copy. If I want to see you try this recipe for Workforce Optimization, I know I can't leave out the single most important ingredient: a tool that supports the business practice! I like to think of it as "TNT" "Techniques and Tools." Now isn't that clever?

If we're going to look at training results levels three and four, then we need a way to gauge true impact on job performance, and the impact of job performance on output, and the impact of output on profitability. Now you'll see why earlier we spent the time to discuss the areas of a company. As the company defines the company goals (most often written and targeted in terms of higher financial results, but one step down) it gives us the final goal of any personnel development event. (For both our sakes, from here on out I'm going to just call them "training events" but we'll both know that we really mean any event or circumstances we put someone in that is done to stimulate a person's ability or attitude.) Let's use as a working example the goal of increasing diversified market share by 20%. There's an implied link to higher profitability and/or lowered risk, which is a factor of sustaining profitability. As the company specifies the broader goals, they will by need, be forced to develop or use existing measurements that gauge the company's progress towards that goal. So now we have the company's "Customer Diversification Index" measurement. We've already talked about how the business units will then create the ties to that goal and its measurement to their departments and what they do in their jobs. They will define the job tasks that affect the "Customer Diversification Index." Now the Workforce Optimization team takes the ball and starts to run with it. We build the definition and links between the job tasks and the training events that enable someone to better perform them. All of this is review, but I wanted it fresh in our minds.

At this point we conduct training events and we need to check levels three and four impact. While one way to check this is to look at the job performance of the course graduates, that's a great piece of analysis, but let me introduce a more complex reality. The real need is to look at job performance **within the framework of peer groupings**.

What I mean by that is this, if I look just at Bob's job performance before and after a training event (remember, that term is used to represent our broader meaning) and I see that Bob improved by 10%, should I be happy or not? 10% sounds good, but it still doesn't have any meaning. It only begins to gain meaning when I look at the job impact of everyone who completed the training event. What if the average improvement was 4%? Now I'm really happy with Bob! What if the average was 70% Now Bob's not looking too good, is he? So when we look at levels three and four for impact and the ROI of training events, we need to look at the results in context.

But guess what, I think you already knew that. It's no great epiphany to check results in the context of all those who completed a training event. Well, that is for most people, but I guess when someone is new to real-world Training and Organizational Development it may not be as obvious as I'm thinking you think it is.

But now I'll raise the bar! Perhaps it's to a height that some or most of you have already tried to raise it too (meaning you already know you need to look at things in the way I'm about to describe) or maybe it's a new height that some of you haven't even thought of, but I will venture a guess that it's a height that few of us are trying to clear. I'll admit that for many years it was something that I wanted to be able to do but couldn't find a way to do, so I sort of gave up. Well, only sort of, because I applied the motto of Admiral Perry, the man credited to be the first to the North Pole *"Find a way or make one!"* Here we go . . .

While it's great to look at what happened in terms of job performance as it relates to a set of training event graduates, what if job performance is also affected by the tenure of the participants? What if the real factor is really the work shift on which the graduates then go back and work on? Now we start to see the complexity of the analysis of levels three and four!

So back to Bob and the class he just finished. What if Bob has 2 years tenure, and the average improvement of the 2 year tenured graduate is 4%, while the 4 year tenured graduate average improvement is 18%, now Bob's 10% improvement has its truest, most accurate meaning. We can accurately congratulate Bob on beating the average improvement of his peer group, provided it transfers into lasting improved job performance ...

WARNING!! WARNING!! **DANGER!!** DANGER!! **Don't go crazy with this!**

It's very possible to drive yourself over the edge with all of the factors that could affect job performance! The key thing to always keep in your mind is Workforce Optimization Maxim #5: Consider what peer groups exist that could affect results and check them.

It makes sense that there are some groupings that fall into place naturally (job tenure, class graduates, etc.) and sometimes you have to think creatively (people who speak multiple languages, people who studied in History, etc.) Some possible peer groups that have been found to have an effect on job performance are:

> **Workforce Optimization Maxim #5**
> **Consider what peer groups exist that could affect results and check them.**

(there are no rules as to which way the peer groups work better or worse, its that these are the ways employees are grouped that will affect job performance)

- work schedules (e.g., look at avg. perf. of day shift vs. night shift)
- managers (some coach better than others ...)
- work history prior to your company (don't be deceived by looking for like experience either – sometimes it's just the opposite!)
- work history at your company

- age (sometimes younger people perform better, sometimes more seasoned people perform better – no rule of thumb, just consider if it's a factor or not in what you're analyzing)
- physique (no, not sexy or hunky, but strength, endurance, even ability to sit or stand for lengths of time)
- education (sometimes you think it's necessary and it's not!)
- married vs. single, parent vs. not
- favorable vs. unfavorable last review
- work environment
- I've even heard people try to isolate areas of origin (e.g., a good "Northeast of the US" work ethic)

The only rule of thumb I can give you on analyzing job performance for levels three and four impact is that you have to analyze employees by comparing them to their peers, as closely and in as many different ways as possible. I guess there is another rule of thumb: once you've looked at it three of four different ways, stop – that's far enough! Use it and move on before you're crazy like me.

Once again, I think you need P.E.R.F.O.R.M. to do this, that's why I'm giving it to you! What a colossal self-serving something or the other I'd be if I gave you all this build up and then told you that you have to spend an arm and a leg to get the tool that supports this approach!

In some ways, I think everything before this was just a way to lay the groundwork for what I really want to focus on, and what P.E.R.F.O.R.M. really enables: PEER GROUPING JOB PERFORMANCE ANALYSIS!! I think you're really gonna love this part!

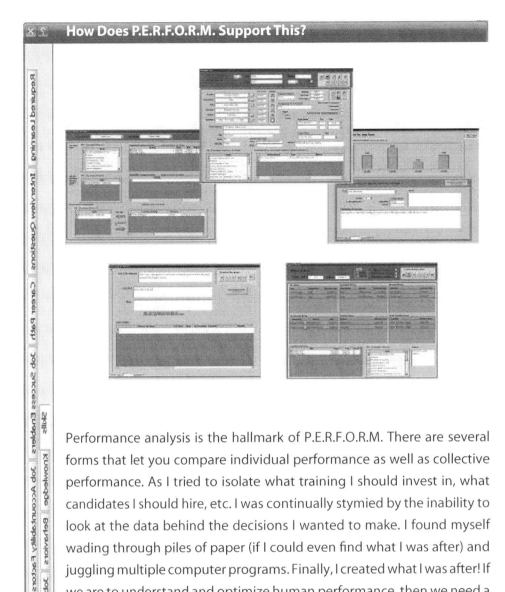

Performance analysis is the hallmark of P.E.R.F.O.R.M. There are several forms that let you compare individual performance as well as collective performance. As I tried to isolate what training I should invest in, what candidates I should hire, etc. I was continually stymied by the inability to look at the data behind the decisions I wanted to make. I found myself wading through piles of paper (if I could even find what I was after) and juggling multiple computer programs. Finally, I created what I was after! If we are to understand and optimize human performance, then we need a tool that lets us look at all of the factors that affect that performance, and it has to be robust enough, and easy enough to use, that it is practical. I believe P.E.R.F.O.R.M. is that tool, or at least a good start at one that will serve all of us as we endeavor forward in our profession. By having these analysis forms, finally we will be able to identify top performers more effectively, and based on a wealth of empiric data not subjective opinion. We can look at employee job performance for individuals and also compared to their peers!

By the way, one rule that I took into this software development project is that the data that supports the analysis screens must be collected easily and for multiple purposes. For example, you'll recall that we collected training registration in one area of P.E.R.F.O.R.M. As we are considering how a top performer became a top performer, one key piece of data is the history of training received. Because we collected registration information as we went along, we now have it at our fingertips to use in our analysis.

As I unveil the analysis forms, the one I'll start with is the one which I find I use the most. It is the one which lets me compare one employee's job performance, for multiple factors, against his/her peers, even for a specific moment in time. If you'll recall, you saw this one at the very beginning. It is the Peer Comparison Worksheet.

Required Learning | Interview Questions | Career Path | Job Success Enablers | Job Accountability Factors

Skills | Knowledge | Behaviors | Job Task Performance Measurements

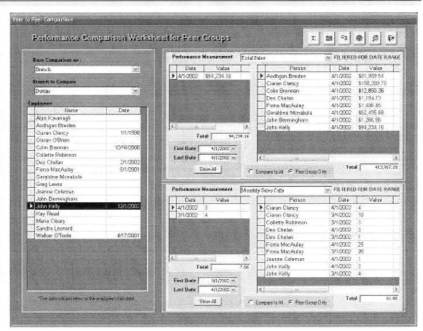

P.E.R.F.O.R.M. Screen– Performance Comparison Worksheet For Peer Groups

Although you've seen this screen before, way back in the beginning of our little recipe book, I didn't take the time to explain all of items on the screen then. Let me rectify this oversight now:

Here is an explanation of the fields, buttons, and tabs on this form:

Item Name	What It's For
Base Comparison On pick list	This is the primary driver for the data that is available in the rest of the form. When you first open the form, this is the only field that displays. Until you choose a basis for your comparison, no other controls will display. This is how you identify/ choose the peer grouping that you want to analyze.

	The entries for this pick list are determined by the entries in the Peer Codes table, described in this section. Some standard peer groups are in the list when you first receive the software, but you may define others as you find peer groups that interest you.
"XZY" To Compare pick list	The label for this pick list and the list itself will change based on the primary peer grouping you've just chosen. If you chose to analyze all those who have completed a course (you chose "Learning Experience Graduate" from the *Base Comparison On* pick list), then this will be a list of all the courses in your course catalog section of P.E.R.F.O.R.M.

Employees list	This is the list of all employees who are in the peer group you have chosen.
	If you double-click on an employee's name in this list, you will open his/her profile. You might use this if you see a performance indicator to the right (we'll get there in a minute . . .) and want to see that person's full background. There are buttons across the top that let you display key elements of a person's background, but you may want to see all of them at once by looking at the profile.
	Depending on the peer group, the Date column will mean different things, e.g., for L.E. Grads, it is the date the person took the class. For the tenure peer groups it is their hire date or their job position start date. Whatever the date means will be displayed in a tip just below the *Employees* list.
	To the left of one employee in this list will be a small, solid arrow. This indicates the single employee in the peer list on which P.E.R.F.O.R.M. is focused. You change the focus by clicking one time on a different name, or using the Up/Down arrows on your keyboard. This will have more meaning in just a moment, when we get into performance indicators.

Required Learning | Interview Questions | Career Path | Job Success Enablers | Job Accountability Factors | Job Task Performance Measurements | Skills | Knowledge | Behaviors

Performance Measurement pick lists (there are two measurement sections)	These let you pick the performance measurement(s) you are reviewing. You've chosen a peer group, now you need to see how the group and single employees are performing. Often you will want to compare either the cumulative measurement of two indicators for the peer group or two points in time for the same indicator. (If you want to evaluate more than two indicators at one time, you'll need to use the Multiple Performance Measurements form from the Main Menu.)
Individual Employee Measurements and *Multiple Employee Measurements* sections	As you select a measurement, there are two measurements sections that appear below the measurement pick list. The smaller one to the left is for the single person on whom the peer list is focused. The other area is the measurements for everyone in the whole table of measurements, but you can narrow this list to just the peer group by using the *Compare To All/Peer GroupOnly* radio buttons.

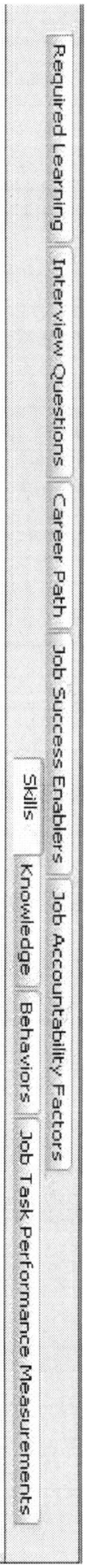

Choosing *Peer Group Only* causes the measurements to filter for just those people in the peer group. This lets you compare one person's results to his/her peer group.

Compare To All returns the list to showing all measurement records in the table for all employees.

Remember – by having many measurement tables to work with you can compare many combinations of choosing a peer group and then a specific set of measurements. For example, you may have Sales numbers for everyone in a table, and then the peer comparison could look at all employees, AND you could have a table of Sales numbers for just a single geographic area. Then the peer group could compare to all in the top section by choosing the measurement table for all the world, and the measurement table for the specific geography in the lower section. It is the combination of peer group AND data that gives this form so much analysis potential! Be creative!!

Compare to All

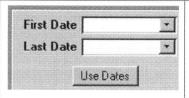

Date selection fields

For each performance measurement area (upper and lower) you can specify a date range for which to filter you data. The list of date choices that shows up is determined by the dates in the table for the measurement you have chosen.

You can use these for the same indicator in the upper and lower, and compare performance for two different points in time (1st qtr one year vs. 1st qtr another year.) When you do this, you may want to use the Calculations form to help you crunch your numbers.

When you click on the *Use Dates* button, your date filters will be applied, and the button will change to *Show All* to let you remove the filter.

If you change the dates, your data will automatically update.

When you use the date range feature, the background for that measurement area will change color (blue) and just above the measurement pick list will be a reminder that you are filtering the list based on a date range.

Required Learning | Interview Questions | Career Path | Job Success Enablers | Job Accountability Factors | Job Task Performance Measurements | Skills | Knowledge | Behaviors

Σ *Open Calculations Form* button	This button lets you open the Calculations form. This form automatically calculates the differences in the upper and lower measurement sections.
Show History buttons	These buttons open different history items for the employee who has the focus. From left to right, they are Learning Experience, Job, and Office history. A person's history displays in the lower section of the measurements area. When you choose to display one of the historical elements, the button used to display it will change to a button to use to no longer display it.
Standard Windows Features are available	Move columns by highlighting them (click on the column header) and dragging and dropping location. Resize a column by highlighting it, pointing to its side border (the mouse pointer changes,) and drag and drop to resize. Sort a single column by a RIGHT CLICK on the mouse while pointing to the column, and then choose Sort from the menu. Sort multiple columns by highlighting them (you may want to move one or more columns first to control multi-column sorting - it sorts left to right by column) then RIGHT CLICK and chose Sort from the menu.

Data Color Coding	In the Performance Measurements form (found on the Maintenance Menu) you specify upper and lower limits for measurement indicators. If someone is below the lower limit, his/her measurement will appear in red. If someone is above the upper limit, his/her measurement will appear in green. If he/she is within the limits, the measurement will be black.

The idea behind this form is the need to understand who are the top performers, which will let us explore how they got to be that way. The only way to truly evaluate job performance is by looking at individuals within peer groupings. Someone may be identified as a top performer, but unless it is compared with how others with similar backgrounds and/or in similar settings performed, we run the risk of skewed analysis and hence, faulty conclusions!

Table Driven Peer Groupings

As you read a few minutes ago, peer groupings are the strongest way to identify and analyze employees who really are your top performers. We designed P.E.R.F.O.R.M. to support your ongoing need to be able to group people by newly discovered peer groups. The Peer Comparison Worksheet is designed to look up in a data table the choices it gives you for your peer groupings, and also, in the same data table, is stored the details as to where that data is found, and how to display it in the worksheet form. The form interacts with a growing data table of definitions so that you never are locked into only those peer groupings we thought of when we designed the software. The peer groups are dynamic and can be added and/or removed as you see a need to analyze by them.

Required Learning | Interview Questions | Career Path | Job Success Enablers | Job Accountability Factors | Job Task Performance Measurements

Skills | Knowledge | Behaviors

Job Task Performance Measurements | Job Accountability Factors | Behaviors | Knowledge | Skills | Job Success Enablers | Career Path | Interview Questions | Required Learning

Keep in mind, one way to manipulate any sort of grouping is by the data tables you create for your workplace results measurements. If I have a table of sales revenue data, but limit the entries to only those employees of Europe, then any peer grouping I use (job tenure, course completion, previous job, etc.) to select the names of people to then use to lookup values in the Europe Sales Revenue data table will already

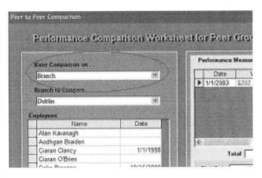

be filtering by TWO peer groupings. Analysis is a combination of the form you're using AND your creative use of the data you store in the tables behind the form.

Ok, back to table driven peer groupings . . .

If you look closely at the sample screen shot above, you'll see that the Peer Comparison Worksheet is filtering based on a grouping based on those employees at the same **branch**. If you were to look behind the scenes into the data tables, you'd find a table entitle "Peer Codes," and in that table you'd find the entry that defines how this form knows what to build for you in terms of a peer grouping based on the branch the employees work at. I'll show you in a minute how a P.E.R.F.O.R.M. database support person can easily create a new reference, but first I just can't help showing you the code that's in this table (I'll use the "By Branch" peer group for our example, so it's the top row in our picture below – I wanted you to see a few others too, so I pasted a look at three of them) so you can see how someone could customize the peer groupings they want.

You start by giving your peer group a name ("Branch" in our example), a little bit of programmer-speak code references, column details, and then a name you'll recognize. You can even specify what the corresponding date you're going to display will represent (in a minute we'll tell P.E.R.F.O.R.M. where to find the date we want to use in the stored measurements data.)

Peer_ID	Peer_Type	Row_Source	Colums_Count	Column_Width	List_Width	Caption	
4 Branch		SELECT Branches.Branch_ID, Branches.City, Branches.Office FROM Branches ORDER BY Branches.City;	3	0,3000,3000	6000	Branch to Compare	E
5 Prior Job - Other Company		SELECT Distinct Employee_Prior_Jobs.Prior_Job AS [Prior Job] FROM Employee_Prior_Jobs ORDER BY Prior_Job;	1	3000	3000	Prior Job to Compare	
6 Manager		SELECT Empl_ID, Full_Name AS [Manager's Name] FROM My_Team Where Mgr_Flag = -1 ORDER BY Full_Name;	2	0,3000	3000	Manager to Compare	F

Don't get blown up by the programming language used in the Row_Source column, it's a worldwide standard known in the computer programming world as Structured Query Language (SQL) which, if your company doesn't have someone who already knows it, contact me (web address is at the very end of the book) and I'll help them (or you) master it.

Here's a look at the rest of the row of data from the peer definitions table that the Peer Comparison Worksheet uses to know how to present a peer group based on the employees' branch . . .

Doubleclick_Form	Form_Lookup_Criteria	Peer_Code	
Branches	[Branch_ID] = [Forms]![Measurements_For_Peers]![Compare_ID_Ref]	SELECT Distinct My_Team.Full_Name, My_Team.Empl_ID, My_Team.Hire_Date AS [Date] FROM My_Team WHERE Branch_ID_Ref =[Forms]![Measurements_For_Peers]![Compare_ID_Ref] ORDER BY My_Team.Full_Name;	*The refers empl
		SELECT Distinct My_Team.Full_Name, My_Team.Empl_ID, My_Team.Hire_Date AS [Date]	*The

Wait! There's two more . . .

Peer_Caption	Source_String_Multi
*The date column refers to the employee's hire date.	My_Team WHERE Branch_ID_Ref =[Forms]![Measurements_For_Peers]![Compare_ID_Ref]))) ORDER BY Full_Name, Date DESC;

When the Peer Comparison Worksheet gets done reading all of that code in the table, it knows where to find what it needs, how to cross-reference and link it, and then how to display your peer group list so it makes sense when you look at it!

When you discover, in your real world, a new way you want to analyze a group of people, all you have to do is figure out how you'll know the group you want by thinking through the real-world combination, and then your P.E.R.F.O.R.M. support person will go into the table and create a new row that gives the Peer Comparison Worksheet the information it needs to display what you want. The point I'm trying to stress is not that it's easy, because it can be complicated to figure out the code, but more so that it is CUSTOMIZABLE!!! ANY peer group you want to analyze can be created without having to hire RSM Solutions, and also without having to reinstall the P.E.R.F.O.R.M. software on everybody's computer!

Finding And Hiring The Best Possible People

Identifying Your Perfect Candidate

Ok, we've looked at what we would gain if we knew who our top performers are and their background to get there, now we can start using that knowledge to help us get them faster! It's time to put our Workforce Optimization analysis of top performers to good use! The fastest way to get top performers is to hire the type of people that become them. However, I've seen many situations where a company **thought** they knew who the best candidates for the job were, and when we looked at the performance measurements of the current workers, and then dissected the background of the top performers and those who reached peak faster, the old assumptions just didn't hold up. Let's just agree that it's easier said than done.

There are two commons assumptions about hiring: hire someone who's done the job; hire someone with a college degree. Sometimes these assumptions are accurate, sometimes they're not. One would have to look at the objective measurements to find out . . .

One of the benefits of a Workforce Optimization environment is that you not only track each person's job task performance, you also have a rich history of many of the elements of their background that made them who they are. If you look at the trends of people who are in similar jobs and establish an average performance level, and then the average time it takes a person to real a point where his/her performance is at that level, then you've set the stage to determine who your perfect job candidates are. You have to know what "average in class" is before you can know what "best in class" is.

Simply put, a "top performer" is one who beats the averages, either one: average time to potential or average performance level. Be careful, though, you have to compare apples to apples and oranges to oranges. That means you have to consider the background of the people you're comparing when looking at time to potential and you have to make sure you are comparing people in as close to the same work environment as possible (similar is ok) when analyzing top performers on the average performance element. Once you know your analysis is sound, then you can look at who beat the averages, and they are your top performers. This peer group becomes instrumental in fulfilling many aspects of Workforce Optimization.

When you invest time and money to develop your workforce, you should consider the ROI on getting your top performers 10% better versus the same time and money invested on the average (or below) performers. The same investment will yield much higher results. Now that doesn't sound like a good "warm-and-fuzzy" HR guy at all, does it? That's because without sound return on investment we won't have the funds to complete the rest of the story. It's unrealistic to think you could have a workforce of only top performers. By the very nature of the label it requires something to be "top" when compared to! So that puts us squarely in reality again. We will still invest time and money to develop average and below average workers, they're part of the family too, I just want us to be clear on the point that it's ok, even a good idea, to invest in your top performers. The top performers are who will primarily drive your company forward!

Now for one of the other benefits of identifying your top performers, our topic of recruiting. It stands to reason that, if I know who my top performers are, then I should try to find others like them. That leads me to a profile of my ideal job candidate. One caution before I go further: keep in mind the benefits of a diverse employee base. I'm NOT advocating your create a group of identical employees! Now for what I am recommending. I recommend you determine what the skills, knowledge, and behaviors are of your top performers, and then go recruit people who have those traits. It's not rocket science, but it is somewhat hard to do, unless you have a tool you can use to help you out . . .

The best way to think of how P.E.R.F.O.R.M. supports this is to first realize that there are several ways to look at employee job performance, and hence identify top performers.

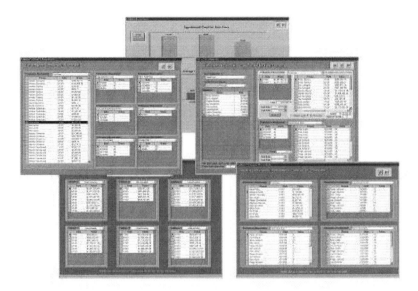

Once you've identified a top performer, then by simply double-clicking on their name in whatever form is being used will open the history file for that person. As the employee's demographic information changes over time (new job, manager, location, etc.) the change is recorded in the Employee Information form. The latest information is always displayed, but the history of the key elements is available with one click.

P.E.R.F.O.R.M. has a maxim of its own: if someone has taken the time to input data once, then use it as many times as possible!

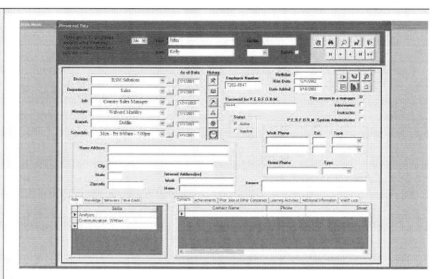

P.E.R.F.O.R.M. Screen– Employee Personal Data

Here is an explanation of the fields, buttons, and tabs on this form:

Item Name	What It's For
Demographics picklists (Division, Department, Job, Manager, Branch, and Schedule)	These let you specify a particular value for that element as it applies to the employee chosen. As an element is changed, you will be prompted for the date on which the change took place. As changes are made, the current information appears here, but every change is stored in a history file for the employee. You can access the history for each element by using the corresponding button to the right of each demographic element.

This Person Is check boxes (Manager, Interviewer, Instructor, System Admin.	When a person's is flagged as being a Manager, his/her name will then appear in the Manager demographic element pick list.
	Interviewer flag adds them to a pick list over in the Job Candidates form.
	Instructor flag adds them to the instructor pick list over in the Course Details form, individual class session list.
	The P.E.R.F.O.R.M. System Administrator flag is **VERY DANGEROUS**. **This flag grants all rights to this person.** Only a System Admin can make someone else an admin person.
Status Indicator radio buttons	While the field is obvious, what happens when it's chosen is not, at first. When you set someone to Inactive, a Date field will display to let you specify the date on which this person became inactive.
Skills, Knowledge, and Behaviors section (those tabs at the bottom left)	This displays these elements as they have already been credited to this person, and lets you add them one at a time, from the full list available.
Misc. Info section (all those tabs at the bottom right)	These just let you record pertinent information. I think they're self-explanatory, but if not, contact me and I'll explain them.

Watch Lists tab	Ok, this one isn't self-explanatory, so I'll explain it. This tab lets you put this person on up to six different watch lists, as defined in the Watch Lists form (from the Maintenance Menu).
	Putting someone on a Watch List causes his/her name to be included in that peer group when it is chosen in the Peer Comparison Worksheet. This lets you create up to six custom peer groups for use later in performance analysis.
	Tip – As a Trainer, I created a Watch List for those learners that I thought had star potential and one for those that I was worried would have sub-standard performance. I was then able to go to the Peer Comparison Worksheet and check on my list of concerned parties (both good and bad concerns) very easily.

(Left margin tabs: Required Learning | Interview Questions | Career Path | Job Success Enablers | Job Accountability Factors | Skills | Knowledge | Behaviors | Job Task Performance Measurements)

Find Employees Who Meet Criteria button	This button opens a form that lets you specify many criteria points for which to find matching employees. You might use this if you wanted to fill an open job position with an existing employee, and want to find those most qualified. Filtering is discarded when the form is closed. Note – Filtered or unfiltered, **you can change the order** (**sort**) in which employees are displayed when you move from one record to the next. Simply move to the field which will be the basis for your sort (maybe Job) right click your mouse button, and then choose Sort from the menu.
Form Reset button	This resets the Employee Demographic form and shows all employees, just in case you just used the Find Employees Who Meet Criteria button but now want to look at everyone.
Open Profile button	This button opens an Employee Profile form that displays all historical information for all demographic elements.
	View Performance Reviews button
View Interview History button	If you want to see who interviewed this employee back when he/she was a job candidate. Interviews are recorded in the Job Candidates form, from the Main Menu.

Required Learning | Interview Questions | Career Path | Job Success Enablers | Job Accountability Factors | Job Task Performance Measurements

Skills | Knowledge | Behaviors

View/Record Days Out button	In the Maintenance Menu, you can access a form that lets you specify vacation and sick leave accrual rules. As an employee is out, this button lets you open a form that documents those days out and the reason. It also displays how many of those types of days the person is entitled to based on his/her tenure against the accrual rules for the company.
View/Edit Learning Experiences button	While the employee's Learning Experience history is displayed on a tab in the bottom right Misc. Info. Section, and you can access a specific registration by double-clicking an entry there, this button lets you access the registration system, filtered for records specific to this employee.
View/Edit Compensation button	It's obvious what area this button opens, but I wanted to note that this information is only for job performance analysis and not for payroll purposes!

Since a company needs to have the latest demographic information for its employees, then someone is going to enter that into a computer. But, as time goes by, those individual updates create a rich history.

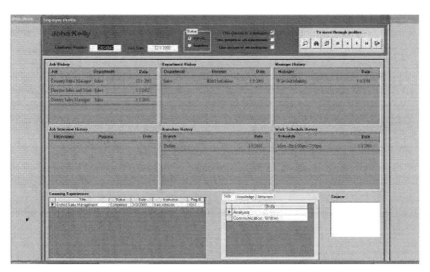

P.E.R.F.O.R.M. Screen– Employee Profile (History)

As well, those who support Training and Development need to have accurate information as to who is signed up to participate in a class, and so someone is going to enter registration into P.E.R.F.O.R.M. for that use.

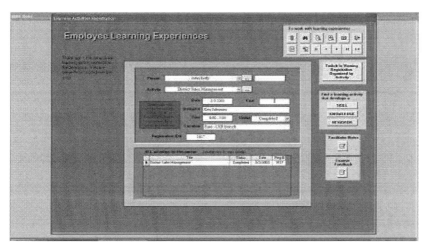

P.E.R.F.O.R.M. Screen– Employee Learning Experience Registration (Individual)

Here is an explanation of the fields, buttons, and tabs on this form:

Item Name	What It's For
Person pick list	This lets you specify for which employee this registration is related. If you double-click the person's name, it opens his/her profile.
Activity pick list	Activities are listed with the session dates, so that one choice from this pick list will populate all of the other fields. If you double-click the activity title, it opens the Course Details.
All Activities section	These are the other learning experiences that this employee is registered for, past or future. If you double-click the Date or Reg # for an item in this list, you switch to viewing that registration entry.
Facilitator Notes and Learner Feedback buttons	Each individual registration has with it areas for the registrar to note additional information.

However, as time goes by, those individual registration entries create a rich history of each employee's development plan, past and future! By the way, whenever you have to serve in the role of "Registrar" for learning events, P.E.R.F.O.R.M. also has a registration screen that enables you to register multiple people at one time.

Job Task Performance Measurements

Job Accountability Factors

Behaviors

Knowledge

Skills

Job Success Enablers

Career Path

Interview Questions

Required Learning

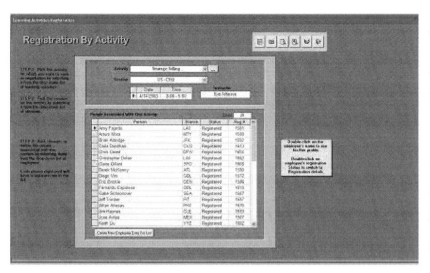

P.E.R.F.O.R.M. Screen– Employee Learning Experience Registration (Group)

Here is an explanation of the fields, buttons, and tabs on this form:

Item Name	What It's For
Activity pick list	You choose the event for which you wish to view/edit information. Choices are those for which details have been entered in the Course Details from (from the Main Menu.)

Once you choose the Activity, the Session list will populate with sessions specified through the Course Details form.

You can choose from the list or start typing and it will fill the field with the first matching item.

Double-clicking the Activity title will open the Course Details for the course. |
| *Session* pick list | Once you specify a session, the registration will appear. |

Item Name	What It's For
Registrants list	As you add people to the list, individual registration records are created for each. You can view/edit a person's registration record by either changing the information in this list or by switching to the individual registration first.
Course Forms	To have a registration list either for your reference or to use for sign-up during the class, simply click on any of the PRINT buttons at the top right.

Recruiting Your Perfect Candidate

When a job opening becomes available, there are two sources from which it can be filled: internal and external (no kidding?!) What we're looking for when we recruit is the best person to fill the position with the least possible development. Since we already know what we're looking for in an ideal candidate, because we did the analysis of what are the traits of our top performers, now all we need to do is to find them. In other words, "the person who will get up to speed the fastest and then perform at the highest level the longest." That's who we're looking for! But how do you know who that is? At this point a harsh reality sets in as we look for people who match our ideal candidate profile. Reality forces us to admit that it's just about impossible to find anyone who matches our profile!! But all is not lost! There's a way to get from where we find ourselves in reality, a pool of limited talent people, to where we want to be, an employee base of top performers.

Ok, great, we need to be able to predict what type of person will turn out to be this perfect candidate, so how do we do that? Well, the best way to predict who the perfect candidate is to look at who your best candidate was. When you go to recruit, you need a profile of what to look for, but base it on analysis of your current superstars, and your current, or hopefully past, under performers. So your first step in recruiting your perfect candidate is to profile what they look like. As well, you also need to profile where they are typically found. To make it easy, here is a good list of the elements to consider in setting your job profile:

1. Work history. Not every job is best done by someone who's already done it. Sometimes you need someone who's done a job that builds a characteristic that helps in performing the job you're trying to fill. For example, a great Sales person may be someone who maintains the card catalog at the library because that job teaches them to be organized (if he/she has other elements endemic to a good Sales person) and being organized is an essential part of success in Sales.
2. Work experience. It's similar to work history, but a slight enough variation to have its own entry. Ask yourself should this be someone's first job? If so, then you'll recruit from those pools. If it's not, then don't recruit at college job fairs!

3. Education history. This is sounding like a typical recruiting profile checklist, but that's only in terms of the elements, not how I'm suggesting you use them! When I think of education, I'm not thinking of direct skill & knowledge acquisition. You may find that a perfect candidate for your job turns out to be someone who attended multiple schools while they were growing up, because they had to learn adapt quickly over and over.

4. Life situations. Not just married vs. single, but where are they from and what do they do. Sometimes it takes a "morning person" to succeed in a job, sometimes it takes a "night owl."

5. Hand in hand with that are hobbies and interests. These help you discover the person's innate behaviors!!

As you have a job opening, you'll then go out and fish in the right ponds for the types of fish you want to catch. The key to success here is to look for patterns in your top performers, but look at the elements with a creative attitude (like the education background example.) Look "between the lines."

It may seem like it's so obvious it shouldn't need to be mentioned, but remember you're going to need to have a way to look through all of your job applicants for those who have a high level of match to the job traits you're after. Just fishing for the right candidate is only part of the chore, being able to put your hands on their application is a necessary part too!

Before we get into how P.E.R.F.O.R.M. can support recruiting, let's get something out that we've discussed before, and make a critical connection within Workforce Optimization theory. I want to bring back on the table our discussion of what leads to an employee being successful in his or her job. You'll hopefully recall that first we have to consider that the employee is just an element within a larger system, the company. So one of the things that impacts success is how the company is using the job's role within the larger company structure. One needs to look at how the position interacts with other positions in other departments, how staffing levels are handled, what tasks in the work processes are handled by this position and how communication and other hand-offs are facilitated to and from this position, etc., etc., etc. In other words, if the job does not have a good fit in the larger ecosystem of the company, even the most stellar worker will still achieve only marginal results, and will, thereby, only be considered a marginal success.

With that said, then we look at the other main ingredient of success, the person him or herself. A person needs to have the maximum personal toolset in order to achieve the best results, and be awarded the label of a "success." We've talked about the components of that toolset in two categories: ability and attitude. I want to discuss this again, because there is a key relationship between recruiting and success based on this dissection of criteria for success. When we go looking for someone who most closely matches our ideal candidate, what we are really fishing for is someone with the same skills, knowledge, and behaviors. Remember, "behaviors" was my label for what people "are" and skills gets at what people "do." Knowledge is more of an enabler in the same vein as skills. Another way to think of them is that skills and knowledge determine what a person **can** do, behaviors determine what a person **will** do.

And now we want to recruit someone! My suggestion is that you prioritize your recruiting wish list and place behaviors higher on the list to look for. Why? Because you can enable someone in the areas of skills and knowledge much easier than you can alter someone's behavior! Fundamental changes in behavior can be achieved in adults, but the process is far more difficult and protracted than to pass on knowledge or develop a skill. As well, as we detailed in the earlier section on job tasks, natural traits, resulting in innate behavior, will result in faster time to mastery and higher success levels.

If you think about it, the people who best use root cause analysis skills are those people who have analytical personality types. The people who best use oral communication skills are those people who have interactive personality types. Do I need to go on? The times when I have most pulled my hair out both as a Manager and as a Trainer are those times when I'm trying to help someone do a job task that requires the application of a skill that is in conflict with their personality type. It's slightly different than have an intrinsic reward (a good feeling) when doing a job that fits with your personality (motivational fit) it's more like having to do a job that requires you to cut yourself with knives everyday. It's just a bad idea.

And so, my advice is to remember this when it's time to recruit! Look for the personality traits (the behaviors) needed for the job as of higher importance to locate than someone with a particular skill or knowledge. The individual job tasks will require specific personality traits (e.g., attention to detail is required for people who will do document review) and you'll look for those candidates who have those job task specific behavior traits, and you'll also recruit for those who have the aggregate personality traits (e.g., being an extrovert might be necessary because of a high level of people interaction.)

It may seem like a given that someone who is successful at a job in one company would automatically be successful in the same job at your company. Don't be fooled! I have. Learn from my mistakes! The factor of the fit of the job within each of the companies is enough of a reason for caution, but also consider that most people are capable of doing a job that they really don't like (because it's contrary to their personality traits) for some period of time. Eventually it breaks.

So when we look at this element of recruiting, once we know what an ideal candidate looks like, we need to make sure we go fishing in the places where we're most likely to find the fish we're after. With that said, let me pose this challenge: is the right fish working at one of your competitors, or, once you realize the importance of the behavior vs. the skill and/or knowledge, is your fish swimming in a totally different pond than you've been fishing in? If Customer Service is a critical behavior element, have you thought of all those places where Customer Service is a "make or break" element? If you found someone who "comes wired" with this behavior, could you retool his/her skills and/or knowledge to be able to adapt to your environment? The key question is "are they a success in their current job where this behavior is essential?" They must be demonstrating an ability to do a job where the behavior is essential or they'll never do it at your company.

Workforce Optimization Maxim #6
Focus on <u>behaviors</u> when you go fishing.

How Does P.E.R.F.O.R.M. Support This?

The best part of having to fill a job opening is that the job is already defined in P.E.R.F.O.R.M. by its skills, knowledge, and behaviors, so you already know which of these you need to search for. As well, since you can look at performance level based on who is currently doing the job, using the Peer To Peer Comparison form, you can see who are your top performers in that job, then, because what background has helped people in that job achieve higher performance, so you know what background to search for as you recruit.

If you're going to recruit from within, because P.E.R.F.O.R.M. keeps track of all of the skills, knowledge, and behaviors possessed by employees (remember, since the learning experience is defined by the s,k,&b's it develops, when someone successfully completes an activity he/she is credited as having the s,k,&b's developed by the activity, so they are now part of that person's profile.)

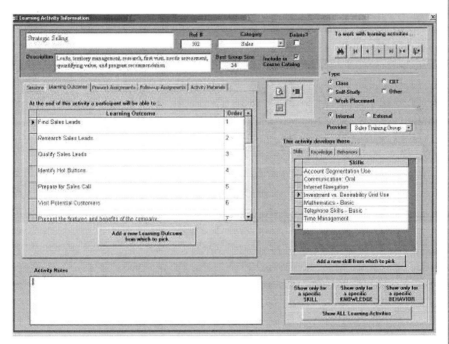

P.E.R.F.O.R.M. Screen–Learning Experience Information

As you look at the Employee Demographics form, you'll see a button in the top right menu area that lets you filter your employee list based on some underlying selection criteria. Guess what that criteria is? All the elements of your Perfect Candidate Profile!

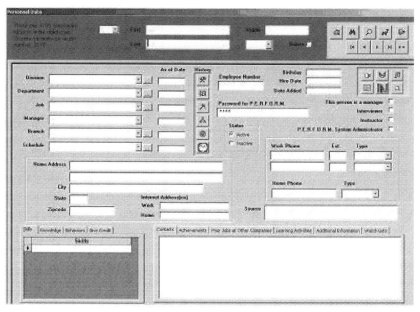

P.E.R.F.O.R.M. Screen– Employee Personal Data

Here's the form above, and here's the filter button.

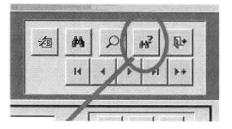

The selection form looks like this:

P.E.R.F.O.R.M. Screen– Employee Background Search

Now you can filter your employee list for any number of criteria! One of more elements, it doesn't matter. Just keep in mind, the more criteria you select, the less your likelihood of finding a match! An employee MUST MATCH ALL of the criteria specified in order to show up in your filtered list. Make sure you really need someone with the profile elements before you get too "criteria selection happy!"

Here is an explanation of the fields, buttons, and tabs on this form:

Item Name	What It's For
Employee Skill pick lists	You can choose from 1 to 4 job skills for which you want to find an employee who has those in his/her background.
Employee Knowledge pick lists	You can choose from 1 to 4 knowledge elements for which you want to find an employee who has those in his/her background.

Job Task Performance Measurements

Job Accountability Factors

Behaviors

Knowledge

Skills

Job Success Enablers

Career Path

Interview Questions

Required Learning

Employee Behavior pick lists	You can choose from 1 to 4 behavior elements for which you want to find an employee who has those in his/her background.
Prior Jobs at This Company pick lists	You can choose from 1 to 4 jobs for which you want to find an employee who has done those in his/her background, or is currently in the specified job.

To fast forward the reading, here is a snapshot of P.E.R.F.O.R.M.'s Job Candidate form (for cataloging résumé's and job applicants.)

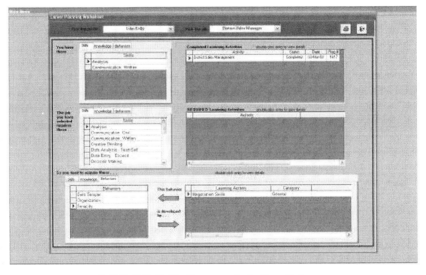

P.E.R.F.O.R.M. Screen–Job Candidates

This area, and it's corresponding form, will enable you to keep track of the people who apply for positions, with particular fields that are related to the key background items that will let you search for the right backgrounds, once you know what background matters for the job you're trying to fill.

Here is an explanation of the fields, buttons, and tabs on this form:

Item Name	What It's For
Source field	I strongly suggest tracking the sources from which you draw your eventual employees. This will give you a terrific bit of insight as you look for future talent. While this is a pick list field, you can also type new entries if you don't find a match. Once you type a new source for someone, that source will now be in the list to be available for picking later.
Interviews area	This is a practical way to keep track of who has been through what stages of your interview process. It will also give you an analysis element later to see what Interviewer has the ability to spot talent and who keeps letting riff-raff into your organization! Use the search form (explained in just a minute), you can search the candidates for those who have been through a specific type of interview (e.g., 2nd interviews only) or have been interviewed by a specific person (the "talent spotter" perhaps!)
Skills, Knowledge, & Behaviors tabs	These are the same elements that are used in your company's job tasks. You will specify that a candidate possesses these by validating them through some method outside of P.E.R.F.O.R.M.
Prior Jobs	While this is a pick list field, you can also type new entries if you don't find a match. Once you type a new job for someone, that job will now be in the list to be available for picking later.

Required Learning | Interview Questions | Career Path | Job Success Enablers | Job Accountability Factors | Job Task Performance Measurements

Skills | Knowledge | Behaviors

 Find Matching button	This button opens another for that lets you find candidates with background elements matching those that fit your Perfect Candidate Profiles!

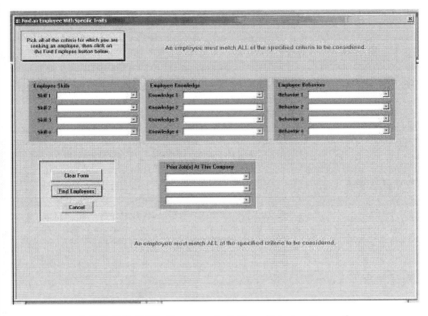

P.E.R.F.O.R.M. Screen–Job Candidates Search

This form works very much the same as the form that lets you find employees who match a specific profile. You can choose any combination of items, but any candidates that P.R.R.F.O.R.M. will suggest must match ALL OF THE ITEMS selected.

Interviewing Your Perfect Candidate

Now for a word about interviewing candidates. Once you know the type of person you're after, and you know the best places to look for them, you have to find out if your candidate matches your hopes and dreams. First, realize that no one is going to be a perfect match, so what you're after is the closest possible fit, and, more importantly, knowing what you're signing up for to get them to where you need them to be (which is fully performing in their job.) That means we need a good way to interview someone to see who and what they are.

A quick reality check tells us that, by the time you come across your perfect candidate, if they're any good at all, they've already learned what the interview forum is all about, and how to look their best within it. That's fundamental interviewing 101. Even when you throw a team interview at them (which I advocate!) they've probably mastered that fairly well too. That makes the interview itself only a fundamental sanity check. In other words, if they can't pass the interview process you REALLY don't want them. But don't worry, even though you can't count on the tried and true interview to give you an accurate picture of your candidate, there's still a way to get a peek behind their mask.

We had an evolutionary leap in the interviewing process thanks to Development Dimensions International's Targeted Selection approach. I'll summarize the concept as ask about a specific time someone did in a past job

> **Workforce Optimization Maxim #7**
> **Past performance is not just the best way to predict future performance, it's the ONLY way to predict future performance.**

what you're looking for them to do in your job. Ask them for specific examples. The theory (and I can personally vouch that it works, having done 1,000's of interviews using this technique!) is that if you ask a hypothetical question ("Would you stay late if the job required it?") you'll get a hypothetical answer ("Of course I would!") If you ask for specific times in the past when the person actually performed a skill or used some knowledge or applied a behavior, then you'll be able to predict their future performance based on their past performance. This is a great way to interview candidates, and wholeheartedly advocate your attending this course (no, I don't get a referral fee.) Past performance is not just the best way to predict future performance, it's the ONLY way to predict future performance. Even skill level evaluation (some sort of job simulation testing, which I also advocate!) will only tell you if a candidate **could** perform the job, not if the candidate **will** perform the job. Remember, attitude is one of the two required factors of a fully engaged employee.

One great outcome of this "tell me about a time" approach is that it will cause you to create and use an interview guide for every candidate. Not only will this help you objectively evaluate candidates, but it'll also keep you out of court. A key criteria to hiring is to evaluate all candidates against the same criteria! Enough on the legal issues, I just want to highlight the great idea of the interview guide.

Having used the aforementioned great interview technique, I still found I made some poor hiring recommendations. I needed something else, something in addition to the "tell me about a time" approach, and I found one. I call this technique "**interviewing between the lines.**" It follows the same logic as job testing to evaluate candidates, only it's not so easy to figure out. What you're going to do is put the candidate through a job test, but not an obvious one. Once again, I'll explain by using an example. Let's say that you've identified tenacity (stick-with-it-ness) as a key behavior of your successful employee. Now you need to determine if your candidate possesses that quality. If you ask them if they're tenacious, provided they know what the word means (it took me 5 years of hearing it before I looked it up in the dictionary!) they'll most likely tell you "sure, I'm tenacious." But how do you know if they are or not? Interview between the lines! In your interview process, make it difficult for them to pursue the position (it usually is anyway!) If they 'stick with it" to pursue the job, the chances are higher that they have the behavior trait know as tenacity. All you're trying to do is ready your probability odds.

Here's another one. Let's say that you've identified that top performers of a specific job need to be good listeners. Don't just ask them to tell you about a time they exhibited that behavior (good), or ask them to summarize something you've said (better), keep changing the subject in the interview and see if they can follow along (best!) If they stay with you then they're probably good listeners.

Of course you'll use an efficient interview process to support all of this:
1. Resume review (looking between the lines too, not just facts)
2. Phone interview (use an interview guide for this too)
3. First interview (usually with an HR professional)
4. Job test (challenge yourself to create one)
5. Team interview
6. Manager interview
7. Internal Customer interview (they will be affected, so they should have a voice)

If you really want to try something revolutionary in the realm of interviewing between the lines, then invite your final round of candidates to attend an all-day training event, and observe how each behaves throughout the day, PARTICULARLY during the lunch break. If you choose the course topic wisely, let's say a course on "Teamwork," then those who make it through this final "interview" will already be started on their development. Or course this approach does skew the candidate pool to those who are free to spend the day in a training class. Sometimes your best candidates are those who's current schedule keeps them from being able to attend. Don't rule them out, but do consider how serious they may or may not be.

Hiring Your Perfect Candidate

The most important element of a good hiring process is to clearly set expectations, both job performance levels (and when they will be reached) as well as skill development and knowledge acquisition. That means that a good hire package will define in what development events they will participate, when, and with what expected outcomes. We never find a perfect match of skill, knowledge, and behavior traits possessed by a candidate and the job he/she will do, so having a good way to catalog each (those the job requires and those the candidate has) will enable us to better manage getting the candidate up to speed against the job requirements.

Keep in mind that P.E.R.F.O.R.M. will let you identify who the interviewers are for each candidate. While this doesn't do much for analysis of the candidates, as time goes by, you'll see a track record for who can spot talent (because their name will show up in the interview history of many top performers) and also who keeps hiring problem employees. Learning from our mistakes is as important as learning from our successes.

Now for the specifics of how P.E.R.F.O.R.M. supports hiring . . .

We've already seen how a job gets defined by the tasks performed by someone who does it, and how those tasks are related to skills, knowledge, and behaviors needed to perform them well, the last piece is to see how a job candidate is matched. Because, whenever possible, companies want to promote existing employees into open positions, (you'll still end up with a healthy number of "outside" people coming into your company even with this internal promotion strategy,) the best place this happens is in the Career Planner form. It can also be documented in a Performance Review form, and or through registering the person for specific future learning events. Let's start by looking at the Career Planning Worksheet form.

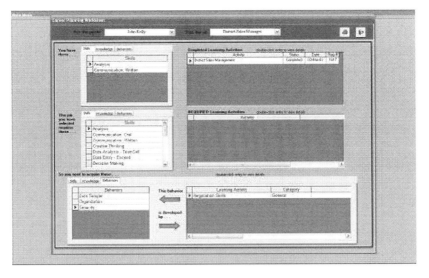

P.E.R.F.O.R.M. Screen–Career Planning Worksheet

Here is an explanation of the fields, buttons, and tabs on this form:

Item Name	What It's For
"Pick The Person" field	This field lets you specify the person for whom you are planning a career advice.
"Pick The Job" field	P.E.R.F.O.R.M. lets you choose a development plan for a person who is in one position to grow into readiness for another position. This field is used to identify the TARGET position.
"So You Need To Acquire These" section	Once the person and the target job have been identified, the form is pretty much filled in for you, but this section is interactive. If you click on a s.k.b. item in the left part, it will show the learning activities that develop it in the right. If you **double**-click on a learning activity in the list, P.E.R.F.O.R.M. will open the details for that learning activity for your to review it's lesson plan.

As someone is looking for a position or is being considered for a new position, the Career Planning Worksheet helps to identify a development plan for that person for the desired job.

As well, the form that catalogs employee demographics, the Personal Data Form, can be filtered to show those employees that match a search criteria. If you open the Personal Data form, and then click on the Filter Employee button , you open a criteria selection form that lets you tell P.E.R.F.O.R.M. the attributes you are looking for. You can specify any combination of items simply by choosing them on the criteria selection form.

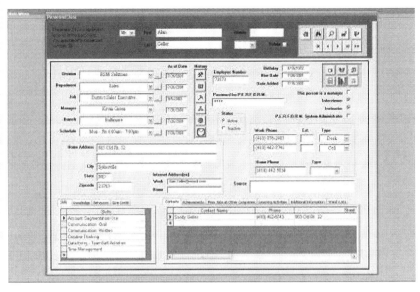

P.E.R.F.O.R.M. Screen–Personal Data form

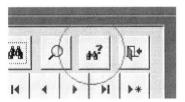

Criteria Selection button

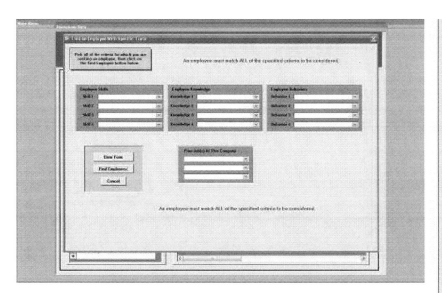

P.E.R.F.O.R.M. Screen–Personal Data Criteria Selection form

All of these items combine to help you recruit, interview, and hire your "best fit" candidates. Holding out for the best fit instead of the best available will help you achieve the maximum results you're after as you look for ways to optimize the employee workforce!!

Chapter Eight:
Aligning Training and Development for Workforce Optimization

- Mulligan Stew . . .

- The Components of Employee Development

- Rule For Identifying Necessary Courses

- Building the Management Plan

- The Learning Forum

- Lesson Plan Steps

Mulligan Stew . . .

There's a dish that was invented in Scotland centuries ago called "Mulligan Stew." It's meant to be a collection of all sorts of leftovers and a few new ingredients that all get blended together into a stew of the tastiest and hardiest nature. When eaten, it can come first in the meal, last in the meal, or even serve as the entire meal. The idea is that it forms the foundation for the entire meal. In that spirit, I introduce the last section of this recipe book: the section that is a collection of a whole bunch of details about the subject of "TRAINING." I believe that training is the foundation for any successful company. While it is only one component in the larger Workforce Optimization disciple, it is the glue that holds it all together. It is the foundation for the learning company's ability to pull off the complex inter-relationships of all of the Workforce Optimization puzzle pieces. It is the "Mulligan Stew."

I've chosen to introduce last this collection of details on lessons learned and collected best practices of successful Corporate Trainers because I wanted to first give you a good introduction to the larger Workforce Optimization world. Could I have started with this section, ended with this section, or made an entire separate book of this section? Yes. But I want to make sure I clearly explain that Training cannot and should not be thought of as a "stand alone" world: it must always be thought of and managed as in integral part of the larger world of Workforce Optimization. However – it is the single most important part, because it is woven throughout and supports all of the other pieces. If we neglect to discuss Training and Development it would be like building an airplane but leaving out the engine! It might look nice, but it'll never get off the ground!

I've learned some things the VERY hard way, and I'm hoping you'll **be smarter than me** and learn from my successes and mistakes, and so I venture into the sections that make up the rest of this recipe book: those focused on what I consider the bulk of my career - Training. I think it was Mark Twain who said, (ever notice how anytime anyone can't remember who said something they say it was Mark Twain who said it, either him or Abraham Lincoln, or maybe Gandhi, or Napoleon, or Confucius, or Alexander the Great, or Julius Caesar, (sorry Peter, I can't think of any Australian heroes to throw in here, maybe Capt. Cook? No, he was British), when all else fails, we claim that it's in the Bible, somewhere,) any way, Mark Twain once said "it's a wise man who learns from his own mistakes, but it's a wiser man who learns from the mistakes of others!" See, all that build up probably ruined the impact of that quote, but Mark Twain probably had something to say about that too. Or was it Lincoln? Oh well, and away we goooo . . .

People Change Slowly

It took me a long time to realize why I wasn't seeing the results I was hoping for with the people I thought I was helping to learn. Then it dawned on me: people learn quickly, but people change slowly! What this means is that the initial grasping of concepts in a "text-book" environment isn't always easy, and there are things we certainly should do to make it easier, but even when the initial

> **Workforce Optimization Maxim #8**
> **People learn quickly, but**
> **people change slowly.**

learning takes place, people have to return to the jungle in order to do these new things. That's where it all breaks down. The pressures and distractions pull even those with the best intentions to change off onto the side roads of performance. How much more those who really weren't that excited in the first place.

If you want to help someone change, work with the "back to the jungle" reality. Consider how you might add "touch points" after the learning experience ends, perhaps at 30, 60, and 90 days, to bring people back to the mountaintop experience, and refresh their resolve and focus that they had when they finished the formal event. Perhaps it's a phone call, card, or email from you, perhaps the same from someone else in the company. I like to use course highlight reminders to the learners, along with a separate note to their manager(s), with some sort of observation and coaching suggestion.

If people learn quickly, we need to help them change faster!

Develop Programs Not Courses

As we even get started, the very first, and "hint, hint" what I consider most important strategy to keep in mind when trying to tackle the specific Workforce Optimization element of training and development of individual and groups of employees is: develop **programs** not courses. As you create formal learning events to stimulate behavior change, keep in mind that one isolated event only has limited impact. When you create a series of learning experiences, targeted at the tasks for each job **role** in the company, you create the framework for optimal development. It's similar to the idea of training in waves, which is presented elsewhere in this book, but slightly different. What you want to create is a complete learning environment where there are learning stimuli coming at the learner from all kinds of different angles and of varied forums, durations, and participants. One might be a series formal classroom events, (people learn more from 4 sessions of 4 hours each, spread out over two weeks, than they do in two 8 hours days spent back-to-back,) another might be a book they are guided through reading, another might be a scripted "chat" they have with a co-worker or Sr. Manager, yet another could be a strategically placed job aid, such as the "Tip of the Day" that pops up when they start their computer in the morning (and I mean something truly useful in job task execution not just some wise old saying.) All of these come together to stimulate faster, more deeper learning. Multiple "touch points" recall what was learned in the formal training while the person is applying it on the job. Recurring learning over time is the best way to bring about behavioral change. If you like to create puzzles, then this is the job for you!!

Think back to when you were young, and the adults in your life used to say to you something like "how many times do I have to tell you something before you do it?" Well, nothing's changed. We're all that little boy or girl who needs to hear something more than once for it to REALLY sink in. That what this concept of a **learning environment**, consisting of learning programs for each job role, is all about. Multiple touch points of learning congeal into faster, more deeper learning. When it's mixed with proper management accountability to practicing what someone has been taught to do, a.k.a an effective Management Plan (more on this later …) then you have created the optimal environment for job performance success!

I should add that at certain stages of tenure employees will have different skill levels, so consider creating development programs that bring into play at the exact right time the learning that matches where their skill level should be, and what will stimulate them at that point to move to the next plateau. Give the full vision of how the skill needs to be performed in the initial event, but then develop the core competencies first, and add complexity in ever-widening circles over time. The timing of when new learning stimuli are introduced is almost as important as the "How are they introduced?" and "Of what nature do they consist?"

With this approach, you begin to develop the foundation of a sophisticated skill in someone's first year on the job, and then introduce the next element of the same skill once he/she has mastered that basic. We've all seen this in practice. Think about the goal of the childhood education system: public or private school. One goal is for children to become proficient in mathematics skills to a level of basic competence. However, you can't start a third grade child off with multiplication of fractions. In the first grade the child is taught how to add and subtract, and then, once those basics are mastered, we add the layer of fractions later. As so on, until, at graduation, a mathematically capable child is released into society, we hope.

The same strategy should be present in our business setting when it comes to developing job skills. There should be a "program" to develop the skill sets necessary for each job role, and that program should take into consideration perhaps even multiple years of tiered instruction.

"Training and Development" Defined

So what is "training and development"? Any Trainer who's worth his/her salt will be able to recite for you (I had to look them up in my notes...) Robert M. Gagne, Leslie J. Briggs, and Walter W. Wager's 9 stages of a learning event, from their hallmark book _Principles Of Instructional Design, Fourth Edition_:

1. Gain attention
2. Inform learners of the learning objectives
3. Recall prior learning
4. Present new information

5. Guide learning (demonstrations should be designed into the courseware)
6. Elicit performance in practices and simulations
7. Provide informative feedback
8. Assess performance
9. Enhance retention and learning transfer

We'll certainly talk about how to manage these, because I think **the learning event is the single most important factor** in an employee's ability acquisition, it may not be the place where the most time is spent, but it is the place that sets the direction and creates the filters of understanding for every experience that follows, but realize that there is more to someone acquiring ability than managing the time and series of learning events themselves. The learning events, managed by Gagne, Briggs, and Wager's 9 stages, are **just a subset of the full employee development effort**.

Instructional Systems Design (ISD) methodology provides the best framework to help understand, and manage, this critical business element known as "training and development" (which I'll remind us is really helping someone **acquire ability**.) The ISD methodology guides us to consider that a good instructional system considers what happens before, during, and after a learning event. I think this is key to helping people acquire ability in an optimal way. If we are to help someone acquire ability, then we need to **map out the entire journey** as best we can, not just the formalized part of their journey. That means we need to "manipulate" things that happen before, during, and after these "mountaintop" moments in time. A good Trainer thinks about what should happen on the entire journey, and then designs all of the pieces to work together for maximum acquisition of new ability. I think the previous chapters of this book, the study of Workforce Optimization, explains how there are multiple factors at work in the company's larger people ecosystem, now let's turn our attention to how best to arrange the journey for those who will travel on our training train.

By the way, throughout the rest of the book, I'll continue to use the term "learning event" to mean the point at which theory collides with reality and someone has to actually step into a setting and help someone know more at the end of their time together than that person did at the start. Since formal learning can occur in many forums, I don't want to just say "class" to refer the moments during which formal, structured instruction is taking place.

So now we are ready to use our ISD framework for talking about learning programs by borrowing from the list of the ISD phases:

Phase One: Analysis

Phase Two: Design

Phase Three: Development

Phase Four: Implementation

Phase Five: Evaluation (control)

ISD Phase I – Analysis

Analysis Phase Steps

1.1 Analyze Job

1.2 Select tasks/functions

1.3 Construct job performance measures

1.4 Analyze existing courses

1.5 Select instructional setting

Analysis Phase Outputs

1.1 a list of tasks performed in a particular job

1.2 a list of tasks selected for training and a list of tasks not selected for training

1.3 a job performance measure for each task selected for instruction

1.4 an analysis of the job analysis, task selection, and performance measure

1.5 construction for any <u>existing</u> instruction to determine if these courses are usable in whole or in part

1.6 selection of the instructional setting for tasks selected for instruction

Inputs, processes, and outputs in Phase 1 are all based on job information. Remember, it is the business unit that executes the business processes that result in products and services that customers buy, so it is the business unit that needs to define the "how to" in the how to do the job task. It may sound odd, but it is often during development of instruction that the specific ways the business unit wants a task performed are decided. When you have to solidify how to teach someone to do something, natural order emerges. One of the valuable benefits a company receives by creating job task training is not the actual trained employee, that's a big benefit, but it is also the analysis of the job itself by the partnership of the business unit people and the Training and Development people. As the partnership of the two groups try to firmly define how job tasks are to be done, the business unit employees often question steps and or procedures, and then find better, more efficient ways to do the job tasks, based on the quest for "process out of chaos."

In every start-up project to develop instruction, I've come across the ever-present "but in this case" types of task execution explanations. Over and over I've found that someone who is really good at doing a job knows all of the times when there are exceptions to how the job task is done to standard, and wants to have all of those instances explained at

> **Workforce Optimization Maxim #9**
> **You can't "train" chaos.**

the moment the new person is learning how to do the job. Knowing them is a great accomplishment, and wanting someone else to know them too is not only noble but also germane to good job execution, the only problem is that trying to pass them all on at once, especially in the early stages of someone learning the new job, is the best way to short-circuit a person that I've ever seen! You simply just can't teach someone both the job task and all of its exceptions all at one sitting. Or even multiple sittings done in a short amount of time. We need to master the basics, and THEN add the complex.

So how do we plan for this strategy during the design and development of training programs? Instead of trying to teach someone complex tasks with multiple variable steps and decision points, try to find ways to pull out of the job task routines and consistencies. **People learn faster if something has repetitiveness and/or "rules" to follow**. If you can reduce what you want someone to master to a process or routine, they can learn to master it faster.

You can introduce variation into the process once the basics are learned, but it's like building onto an existing foundation versus building from scratch. The learning curve is much shorter when someone is adding to an existing knowledge base. When job tasks carry the element of repetition, it soon becomes "behavior" instead of "knowledge and skill," which results in a higher level of performance consistency (less errors!) This technique will probably cause a re-design of the job process, but the benefit of faster mastery, and most likely a residual gain in more consistent quality of performance, will more than offset the time and effort to create routine and process.

Finding the "order" within the "chaos" often requires you to think generically instead of staying focused on each step in the process that the subject matter expert is explaining. You will have to assimilate towards routine, and then play the generic back to the person for validation. For example, when someone tells you all of the criteria they use to determine if a potential customer is credit worthy, as one of the first things they do in selling a product, instead of trying to capture as a training topic all of the criteria, the "order" within all of the "chaos" of multiple criteria is that the process has in it a step to "check the credit worthiness of the potential customer against certain criteria." You can then capture notes on all of the criteria, and perhaps give that to a someone learning the job task as a job aid list. Over time, as they take out the list and use it for awhile, they will eventually, through the amazing ability of the mind to remember rote learning items, they'll learn the list of criteria and won't need the job aid. But the key gain is that for some time you will have them performing the job task, although they need the list, but they're not sitting in a room trying to remember all of the specific details before being to do the task at all.

ISD Analyze Phase Defined

Now on with our task of task analysis. To best understand how a task is performed, an inventory of job tasks needs to be compiled, and then divided into two groups: tasks not selected for instruction and tasks selected for instruction. The standards for those tasks selected for instruction are determined by asking the business unit mangers, or often by observation at job sites (I've even found myself in the field with a stop watch on many occasions!) and then verified by subject matter experts. Remember, it is the **dichotomy of voices** that make learning happen, so deciding what to teach and how the task is meant to be performed should be done with the business unit managers not only so you will know exactly for what to develop instruction, but also so that the business unit manager can later coach and hold accountable, and thusly complete the circle of instruction that leads to behavior change.

As a final analyze phase step, the list of tasks selected for instruction should be reviewed for the most suitable instructional setting for each task. You should start to think of how the task can be taught, and try to address any known time and resource budgets early on in the design phase. It does no good to create a perfect 5-day classroom learning event only to find out that the business unit only has a 3-day threshold of tolerance for employees to be consecutively off task. I'm not saying you forget what you have determined to be the best way to train a task, but you must work within constraints. In this case, you may want to design a pre-work assignment, with a 2-day initial classroom event (it never hurts to exceed expectations!) and then a 1-day follow up field event. I have seen the most fruitful results come when someone is "poked" over time as the implementation of a well designed learning "event." The whole series of interactions are your designed "event." Whether it is through follow up correspondence, or literally multiple meeting times spread out over time, the strategy is the same: remind the person of what they are supposed to be mastering, and then take them a little further. Keep in mind, studies tell us that people only remember 40% or less of what they are exposed to in a learning event. If you spread the learning out over time, and certainly if you send reminder correspondence, highlighting key points from the learning event and how to apply them at the moment, you bring back to the conscious mind what was discussed, and a little more of it sticks and shows up in changed behavior.

There is **a windfall byproduct** to being involved in training course development: you learn how to do the things that your company does to make money!! This pays off later when it's time to deliver the instruction because the higher level of understanding raises your ability to talk though these things at a deeper level, resulting in a credibility boost from your learners, AND it raises your credibility, and resulting respect, amongst the leaders of your organization!!

Rules for Identifying Necessary Courses

Not everything you thing of is something for which you should development training. **Train the high volume tasks!** 30% of the tasks will make up 80-90% of their work week. Teach a learner how to do the 30% of the total number of the tasks they will do in their job, to a level where, when they hit the streets, they can do the tasks at a level = 75% productivity and 95% quality of a fully performing employee. The other 70% of the tasks they will have to learn how to do only make up a small percentage of where they will actually spend their time, so let them learn those as they go along, maybe with some job aids put into place.

When you're considering if you should create a course to tackle what appears to be a company need, consider these checkpoints:
1. You Can't Train Chaos - Train Process
2. Train tasks that get done most often
3. Train tasks that have the greatest payoff
4. Train what is hardest to learn independently
5. Train information that is foundational first
6. Train what has shown most return on investment

The Three Filters

The preceding section assumes one thing: that you are looking at something that should be trained on in the first place! It talks about what to focus training development on, but I want to remind us of what Robert F. Mager and Peter Pipe brought to the table years ago with the hallmark book "*Analyzing Performance Problems, Third Edition*." Not everything that is broken in the workplace is due to something that training can/should fix. I like the widely accepted paraphrase of their concept as the question "can they do this if you hold a gun to their head?" Sometimes people perform below acceptable levels simply because they don't want to do something right. It's not a "training problem" it's a person problem. Maybe the job design itself is contrary to good job performance, like the receptionist at the hotel who also has to field incoming phone calls, someone is going to get less than desirable customer service. Maybe the manager gives the crap jobs to those people who complete them, so the reward for doing a good job with a lousy task is actually the punishment of then getting all of the future lousy tasks. Not really a motivating environment. And sometimes, it's a training issue, they really don't know how to do something.

I used to jump through hoops when I first became a Training Manager, and every problem that I was presented I tried to find or create a training program to fix. Then I read Mager and Pipe's book. I realized that the situation I had bought into was one of the business leaders coming to me with their people and saying to me "this person's broken, fix him." I just jumped to the call and tried to fix him. Then I read Mager and Pipe's book. I started to look behind the performance problem to see what the root cause was, and if it really could/should be "fixed with a training intervention. The question becomes "if they can't perform up to expectations, is it because the person will not, does not, or cannot?" To make it easier, let's just call it "won't, don't, or can't."

To say someone "can't" perform, that means that the person is lacking in some essential skill, knowledge, or task enabling behavior. You can help someone who "can't" perform. You can train and coach someone who "can't" perform.

At the other end of the spectrum of performance problems is the person who "won't" perform the job properly. You find this hidden cause only after you explore the root causes of non-performance and rule out the "can't" factor and then the "don't" factor (the explanation of which is coming next) all you're left with is the "won't" factor. This is the disenchanted employee who has either struggled through both the "can't" and "don't" phases, and finally arrived at a "won't" factor. This person is entirely enmeshed in an attitude problem root cause. You're only hope of correcting this job performance problem is to discuss the cause openly and honestly, and see if you can help them "reset their attitude clock." If you have done all you can to address their concerns, then you must remove this person from your workforce. It may sound harsh, but this is a cancer that will undermine all of your other efforts!

To say someone "does not perform" (don't) is to say that he or she could perform the task, and even implies that he or she wants to perform the task, but, for some reason, does not. This could be due to the "won't" factor, but when the person truly does want to perform the task, and can perform the task, that leads us to the realization that they are inhibited by some factor external to the person. The person who can but doesn't perform their job correctly is most likely hampered by job design issues. Perhaps the workload is such that, to make it through the amount of work required, the person has learned to "take short cuts." Not what you want, but a better problem to have than someone who simply won't perform the job properly. Hey, at least the person is thinking creatively! You'll be able to discern this root cause from the "won't" root cause by the presence of passion in them as they describe what's going on as they try to perform their job tasks. Keep in mind that this person can hold the keys to some incredible business gains as you dig into what he/she perceives to be the barriers to healthy job performance levels. There may be some larger intra-department job design problems that are truly impacting your person's ability to do his or her job tasks. If you discover and address them, you can see significant results. FYI - 20% of all performance problems are due to "don't" causes (70% are "can't," leaving the unpleasant reality that 10% are "won't" problems.)

What I'd like to stop and highlight is the underlying workplace shift that took place in my mind, and that I'd recommend you start out with in your mind. I was looking at these employees as "<u>my</u> wards" and I was going to help them succeed. That's not a bad thing, in fact I'd say it may even be a bit noble to have that perspective. The only problem is that, if I really want to help someone get better, to think of them as "my" wards is a flawed perspective. What really is the case is that they are the business unit manager's employee, and I work on his/her behalf to help him/her help his/her employees get better at doing their job. If we really get down to reality, these employees really are their own wards, and they must help themselves get better at doing their job, but that won't happen most of the time, and so I've come to compromise on the perspective that these employees are the responsibility of their manager, and I'm the manager's internal resource in his/her quest for higher job performance.

So back to the topic at hand: what do you invest training development time in, and when do you invest employee training time? There are three time-tested "filters" for helping you determine if you have an employee with an enablement deficiency, or if you have an employee who just won't do a job task.

Filter One: Should the employee be able to do this? This gets at job design and reward/punishment systems. It also asks the question "is the standard too high?"

Filter Two: Can the employee perform the task in the current environment if he/she is forced? This is another element of job design, but is more focused on the environment vs. the tasks themselves.

Filter Three: Can the employee perform the task in a textbook environment? If they can't, and it's something that can and should be done, then you truly have a training need.

ISD Phase II – Design

Design Phase Steps
    2.1 Begin with the end in mind
    2.2 Identify the building blocks (and describe entry behavior)
    2.3 Build the Management Plan (how the learning fits into the larger workscope)

Design Phase Outputs
    2.1 a learning objective for and a learning analysis of each task selected for instruction
    2.2 test items to measure each learning objective
    2.3 a test of entry behaviors to see if the original assumptions were correct
    2.4 the sequencing of all dependent tasks

When we turn our attention to phase 2, designing instruction, we're really just taking the next logical step to use the job analysis information from phase 1. We'll need to understand the tasks the employee will need to be able to do when he/she leaves the training event, convert those job tasks into learning objectives for our course, determine enabling objectives and learning steps necessary for mastery of the terminal learning objectives, and lastly design tests to match the learning objectives. A sample of students should be tested to insure that their entry behaviors match the level of learning analysis. This is the scope or training design.

To the highest degree possible, the learning environment must reflect the actual production environment. If there is a high level of pressure in the production environment, a high level of pressure must by synthesized in the learning environment (remember our golf tournament analogy.) If the learner will be speaking live with others in the production environment, the learning setting must incorporate this element. Creative design must be applied to anticipate creating the appropriate setting in which instruction will be delivered. Of course the initial setting will be free of the job simulated pressure, but being able to perform the task **in the production** setting is really the goal of the instruction. You must plan for people to practice the skill in an as-close-to-the-real-world setting as possible. The closer your instructional setting matches the future production setting the better the employee's chances are to hit the field running, and to actually be able to do the task in the real world. You won't have to hear the embarrassing puzzled comments of "but I could do it in the training class … " More importantly, the employees entrusted to your care will never have to utter those terrible words!!

As well, as part of design, managing the transfer of learning to the job continues with planning for job support aids. While it would be a wonderful thing if people could record everything they've been told about how to perform their job tasks, that's just not going to happen. Since the goal of the Training and Development group is to assist in mastery of someone being able to do a job task, well designed instruction can also include (and should include) ways to call to mind quickly what the person learned. Job aids can take the shape of reminder charts or diagrams or even posting a sign with an arrow that reads "push button to stamp widget." Think creatively, but remember, we can't clutter the employee (and the workplace) with signs about everything or coffee cups which proudly display the "Keys To Good Project Management." Whenever possible, make the job aid temporary, like an index card of notes that, once the employee engages it over a short period of time, the information is resident, and the job aid can be discarded.

When I use the phrase "job aid" please don't confuse it with "learning aids" or "memory aids." While acrostics are tremendous learning aids, helping people store and recall information, they are not something that is used on the job. I hate to bring them up, but checklists are probably the most common form of a job aid. I think I'd rather see another coffee cup than have stimulated someone to create another checklist, but then again, checklists do have their place.

How People Learn

What I still find magical is how much better people learn when they experience a forum that is a mixture, when passing new information, with small group breakouts, supported by a healthy dash of individual or small group practice exercises. People like to think that they discovered these wonderful new ideas on their own, which is a bit ominous for those of us in the learning profession, but we can salve our hurt egos with the comfort that we know who was the power behind the force . . .

Now there has long been a body of knowledge intended to understand how people learn. From this group of Neuro Linguistic Programming (NLP) we have their contribution of understanding that people learn, primarily, one of three ways:

- Visual – they learn by watching something demonstrated;
- Verbal – they learn by being told how to do something;
- Knestic – they learn by doing something.

I think this is a wonderful bit of insight! It is sometimes misapplied by people who will announce that they "are visual learners, you have to show me," as if any other method simply will not do. Similarly, you get the people who will tell you "unless I try it, I just simply don't get it," as if they're somehow unique in all the world. The truth is that well designed training will bring into the learning process all of these neuro linguistic learning styles. Succinctly put, learning has a high retention level when it follows this flow:

1. Explain how to perform the task being taught.
2. Demonstrate the proper way to perform the task, with commentary as to what you are doing as it relates to what you told them had to be done in step 1 (you'd be surprised at how many people leave the commentary out!)
3. Have the learners try out the new task in an exercise while you watch and give immediate feedback.
4. Once the learners can perform the task correctly once, allow them to practice it correctly multiple times, while you give feedback as needed.

> **The Learning Model**
>
> 1. Tell people what they're about to learn
> 2. Give the big picture
> 3. Pass new information, tied to prior
> 4. Reinforce to validate understanding
> 5. Practice
> 6. Test to validate learning

When you are designing your learning program, if you consider this flow, and the learning styles with which it connects, then all of the learning receptors are used, and acquisition and retention are heightened. The truth is that, while someone may have a tendency towards one type of learning (visual, verbal, or kinetic,) everyone benefits from each type in some way. Then, when all three are used, not only do you hit each person's preference, you enhance everyone's skill acquisition.

Where People Learn

If, in designing our learning program, we're going to be cognizant of the ways people learn, then let's also keep in mind the **places** people learn. **Not all learning happens in a formal classroom**, that's why I keep using the phrase "learning activity" instead of just "class" (which would have been a lot easier for us both!) I often refer to a training class, or formal learning event as "going to the mountain top and becoming enlightened." And then reality sets back in: people have to go back down the mountain and back to work in the fields and trenches. The reality of it though, is that most of what someone will learn that will enable them to perform their job tasks will actually be **learned by doing their job**. They will learn how to do it by doing it right and by doing it wrong. It's like all of things they will acquire is like a giant pyramid, and the formal training is only the tip of the pyramid, maybe 10%, while the bulk of the ability acquisition process is the 90% that sits below.

The nice part about the pyramid, though, that gives me hope of job security, is that it is the tip of the pyramid, the 10% that represents formal training, that **sets the direction** for accurate, more efficient ability acquisition later on when it is applied on the job, and coached. If someone spends just a little time learning in a formal setting **how to do a job the right way**, he/she will master that job far more efficiently, and with greater results, than if he or she just relied on doing the job alone as the way to success.

To be more accurate, the 90% below the top breaks down into two parts: things coached and reinforced by someone, and then those things truly learned by doing. The full picture is that knowledge takes place in a formal setting, this sets the person in the right direction, but then, as he or she is first trying these new abilities on the job, the only place where you can truly master something, there needs to be someone present observing and giving focused feedback, one item at a time. Master one piece before moving on to the next. Remember, that's a key part of Performance Observations/Reviews that was discussed elsewhere in this recipe book?

Anyway, back to the pyramid . . .

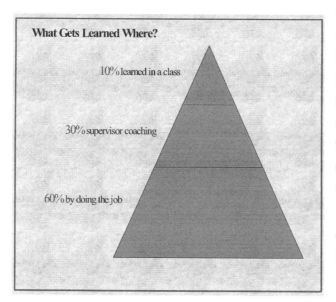

What Gets Learned Where?

10% learned in a class

30% supervisor coaching

60% by doing the job

As I was saying, the most important part of mastering a job is to actually do the job in the real world, and to have good coaching while you're doing it. It's like trying to become a pro tournament golf player. First you go to an expert to learn the fundamentals. The Pro teaches you to keep your head down, arms straight, pull through the shot, bend your knees, etc., etc., etc. ad nauseum, one piece at a time (you master keeping your head down before you focus on bending your knees, or whatever's next.) Then you start playing golf. But the Pro doesn't leave you on your own, no, he or she watches you play and gives you feedback. That's what helps you get your game down! The feedback on how you're performing against the way it should be done, the way you learned in the formal setting.

But you're no Pro yet!

To really learn to be good in a professional game of golf you have to actually compete in a golf tournament! There are factors present when you play in a tournament that you cannot experience any other way than to actually play in the tournament and learn by doing. As you pay attention to what you do, and also perhaps continue to ask for feedback from a coach, you eventually get better and better at playing tournament golf. That's how people acquire ability. The pyramid.

As you design your learning program, consider not just the use of learning events, but also on the job experience before and after as a way to stimulate maximum learning.

Design Phase Step One: Begin With The End In Mind and Formulate the Big Picture

For the training you're developing, it should be tied to enabling some job function. For that job function, decide what task(s) a person will be able to DO when he/she completes the training, or, in other words, what is it they will need to do better when they get back in the trenches. List these in the order they will be performed ON THE JOB. Learners will build their abilities in the same order they will apply them. To help get you in the right direction, list the item(s) out in sentences that start with "At the end of this lesson, learners will be able to …"

Example from a lesson on *Managing a Sales Territory*

At the end of this lesson, learners will be able to:

- Identify the clients that need to be visited on a client call trip.
- Plan the most efficient route for stops on a client call trip.
- Assemble the materials to take on a client call trip.

It has long been recognized that having clearly defined and communicated expected outcomes of a learning activity lead to heightened acquisition and retention. I would refer you once again to Gagne, Briggs, and Wager's book on Instructional Systems Design for an in-depth explanation of writing effective learning outcomes, including enabling outcomes.

Where Workforce Optimization weighs in on this subject is the tie-in to the business unit. At the heart of an effective learning outcome is the focus on what someone will be able to <u>do</u> after the learning activity. A short step from this strategy to where another payoff to managing the forest and not just the trees is to look back to the job design for the tasks required to fulfill a job. These job tasks become the learning objectives for your courses! If a Sales person needs to make phone calls to perspective customers as one of his/her job tasks, then the corresponding learning activity intended to develop that ability would have as at least one of its "learning outcomes" that, at the conclusion of the learning activity, the learner will be able to "make phone calls to perspective customers.' (That was a lot of "learning" in that statement!)

It may sound simple to say the job tasks should be the same as the learning outcomes, but most often there is a disconnect between the two worlds. Reusing the analysis done in constructing the job and its component tasks will automatically create maximum training relevance and learning transfer. As well, since there are already business unit measurements in place to gauge job success, there are then already built in key indicators of learning impact. After all, what does it matter if levels one and two of learning evaluation say things went great but there is no resulting job impact? If you're going to gauge the success of the learning then you're going to need something to gauge job impact. If your learning outcomes are the job tasks themselves, then the method to evaluate level three success will already be available for use.

Performance Environment Check

Also involved in beginning with the end in mind and formulating the big picture is to think of the elements of the production environment and how these affect job performance. The chances are pretty good that you'll have to build these elements into your training plan. If someone has to make sound decisions as a task of a job, and those decisions often have to be made with little time to think, then it's not good enough to just train on the process for sound decision making, you also have to design instruction that teaches them how to go through that process quickly, quick enough to do it on the job!

The last part of formulating the big picture is to think about what drove the initial identifying of the problem you were asked to tackle with some training intervention. Helping to make things better will mean enabling someone do a job task better, but remember job tasks are only done well by fully engaged employees. You need to consider what elements make someone doing these job tasks that we're going to train on more of a fully engaged employee. That means that you're going to need to look at elements that build job relevance, and design into your training event a way to connect that to the tasks you're going to train on. You should also consider what might be obstacles to success of doing the tasks you're training when the employee returns to the trenches, and you should also consider what "outside of their specific world" awareness they should have. All of these elements will show up in one way or another as elements of your training event, but you have to know what they are so that you can proactively design your training with these elements in mind.

> Training Tip: I like to have **an outline** as the output of this step. This is NOT the flow the training event will take, but it's an outline of both the stops on the journey (the larger job functions to be addressed) and the retention and transfer elements that need to be included (obstacles, bigger world awareness, obstacles to transfer, etc.) In the next step we then add the details to the outline.

Design Phase Step Two: Identify the Building Blocks

Once you have the big picture of the work environment and the job tasks to be mastered and documented, the next step is, for **each** task learners will be able to do, list the skills, knowledge, and behaviors (S,K,&B) that combine to enable them to do each one. This isn't a complex step, but it is an often overlooked one. If you're going to help someone get better at a job task, you have to understand the components, and then train on the components. If the job task is to drive nails into a board, then it will require:

Skills
- Nail selection
- Hammer gripping
- Nail holding
- Hand eye co-ordination
- Swing rhythm

Knowledge
- Nail types (size and composition)
- Strike force thresholds (how hard do you hit it before it bends!)
- Nailing angles for various bonding results

Behaviors
- Concentration

Once I see the task details in this structure, now I start to get a better idea of the training I need to develop. But, lest we get focused on just one oak tree (a learning event) let me stop and remind us that it is necessary to consider it within the collection of oak trees (all of the job tasks the Training group needs to support the business in mastering.) If you recall from the example used earlier, if someone may need to know how to read a tape measure in order to cut a board to a certain length, then reading the tape measure is an enabling skill to the learning outcome (and I should add: "job task in the real world".) But also realize that within the "reading a tape measure" enabling skill is another level of enabling skills: working with fractions, or basic mathematics. When running a Training function, optimizing design and development time is a must. To increase efficiency, collect as much details on the job tasks and all of their enablers, and then attack at the level of reusability, such as some learning media that teaches enablers (in this case, basic math) which can be plug and played into multiple courses. As well, someone can complete the enabler for one use, and then not need to repeat it for another use, if you've defined the component enablers and built your courseware for just such flexibility.

At this point of designing your training event, it's time to start thinking about how you will make the content engaging. **<u>After</u>** you know the content that needs to be included, the meat of the course, then it's important to give it some window dressing. Don't fall into the trap of making things corny or campy, or worse yet "training," but rather just shoot for a creative element to the event itself (this is separate from later applying the technique of enterTRAINment.) An example of what I mean by this "make it creative" element, is the first time I encountered this idea, when my boss at the time came back from a training class on accounting. He loved it! I asked him what made it so good and he told me that it was built on sound accounting principles, but then the context of the instruction was that everyone in the class was trying to run a lemonade stand. They taught the accounting principles as they applied to fundamental business practices, but built on the lemonade stand company. The idea was engaging, but it also gave a simple forum within which they could practically apply the concepts. All the rules of running a good business still applied, all of the standard accounting principles still applied, but everyone could understand the needs of running a lemonade stand without the need to go into much detail. It was brilliant – and the concept was creative! That's what I'm talking about with this creative forum concept. It doesn't have to be funny or witty, but it does have to be creative. If you don't plan for it when you're designing the training event, then you'll be left with the same boring format: interactive lectures, small group practices, follow-up exercises. Creative shouldn't be juvenile, it must still be "adult learning," and it doesn't always have to be something to do with the forum. Another idea is to use flash cards to teach rote memory terms. Another is to have a large chart-sized diagram to put out for each small group, and the diagram has different sections that they'll complete as they go through the training event, and then, at the end, you hand out a smaller sized completed diagram for them to take back to the workplace.

My whole point with this is to stop, once you have the content identified, and think of the engagement element. What would make it interesting?

Design Phase Step Three: Design the Management Plan

You're not done yet! Just because you have a very nicely thought out concept of what needs to be learned, that doesn't guarantee success. Before you check off the Design Phase as being complete, you need to spend some time, serious time, thinking about your training event's Management Plan. This is <u>not</u> a plan for how to manage the classroom and/or learners, what I'm talking about here is the one element that will either make or break your training event's impact. You need to know how the business unit managers will support before, during, and after what employees will be learning. It's the **dichotomy of voices** thing again.

"Before the Training Event" Support

We've looked previously at what managers do in their job roles, now it's time to cash in on what they are supposed to be doing. If the manager is conducting regular job accountability reviews, then training needs are going to surface in those discussions. An all-inclusive "management plan" is to have an understanding that employees don't attend training just to check mark off learning hours so you can say you're developing your employees or that "training matters" when you're recruiting new employees or trying to sell to customers. If training has a direct tied to performance deficiencies, then a large part of the management plan will already be accomplished. The employee will have a clear understanding of why they are attending the training event. I REALLY don't like mandatory training events. Something may eventually become mandatory for people new to a job because of a proven track record of heightened performance, but there always needs to be a clear tie to job expectations and employee attendance at a training event. This needs to be part of your management plan. Make sure you have this defined with the business unit managers, and that they communicate it to the employees when they sign them up for the training event.

"During the Training Event" Support

If I could only have one management support wish for "during the training event" support, it would be that they make sure the job is covered so that the employee can focus on learning! To meet this in the middle, I've begun starting at 9:00 and ending at 4:00, just so I can ask people to REALLY focus on what we're training, knowing they will be able to attend to work matters before and after.

Involvement in the event is another technique managers can invoke to support the event. Some training events will be enhanced by having a business unit manager "kick off" the session with words of relevance, others will need at least attendance throughout. Here is where a forum technique we discussed earlier comes up again. If you try to have multiple people involved in the forum, and one or more is a business unit manager, then their participation will heighten the event. This will require more time from the trenches than most managers can in good conscience supply, so you may want to just use "cameo appearances" from these managers. Perhaps have them just come into lead a discussion on application, or maybe to train a short "hard skill."

"After the Training Event" Support

Once again, regular accountability reviews will reinforce the training event, but this aspect of the Management Plan is more short-term oriented. Immediately after the training event, the manager should check to see that what was learned is being applied. This may take prompting from the event trainer, and it may even require a job aid (maybe the same one used by observers during the event.)

I also like the idea of follow-up exercises being administered by the business unit managers. If this can be done through actual work load necessities, then all the better, but at a minimum, there needs to be touch points back to the training event that are instituted or reinforced by the business unit managers.

Since we all have the same goal in mind, helping employees get better at performing job tasks, you can count on management support, provided they see the reason for the actions you are asking from them. As you build your Management Plan for your training event, consider what you need managers to do, and also how you will communicate that need to them well before you put your Management Plan into action.

Higher Job Performance Results Come From Aggregate Planning

One last thought before we leave the design phase and move on to the development of our brilliant instructional program. Consider this equation: good job design = tasks + motivational fit + fast track mastery. In other words, as you work with the business unit managers to design the jobs and job tasks, think about what mastery you can borrow from the readily available workforce, and what elements can be added to the job to tap into readily available motivating elements. Yes, I did say possibly redesigning the job itself! Good ideas regarding how to design a job can flow back to the business unit from the Training and Development group when that means that job performance will be enhanced, and even better when that enhancement comes at little or no cost for instruction!

Maybe this is better explained by using an example. During the days of the Gulf War, I was amazed at the technology behind the very affective "smart bombs." As the Evening News anchor explained how the soldiers guided the bombs to their targets with pinpoint precision, I was quickly struck by the similarities to the guidance system technology and the old video games that many young Americans grew up with. The designers of those systems were able to leverage an existing skill set, with all of its familiarity, to fast-track mastery of their missile guidance technology. Imagine the learning curve they'd face if we didn't have the benefit of a lifetime of training youth through video games. It also has the seeds of a new conspiracy theory.

Now I have no idea or insight into how those two worlds came together, but we can at least learn a powerful lesson from it, whether it was intentional upfront or just a lucky break. The lesson I took from that experience was that, from that time forward, whenever I was trying to help improve the efficiency of a business unit through better job design, I always asked myself the question "is there something we can borrow from the life experience of the average employee to make this job have elements that are either familiar to them or appealing. Even if the job tasks take 10% longer to perform, or it adds 10% more steps, if the job has a faster learning curve or a higher level of engagement, the cumulative effect will be greater performance levels.

ISD Phase III – Development

Development Phase Steps

 3.1 Document learning events/activities (the lesson plan)

 3.2 Document the management plan

 3.3 Review/Select existing materials

 3.4 Develop new materials

 3.5 Validate instruction (sample group)

Development Phase Outputs

 3.1 the classification of learning objectives by learning category and the identification of appropriate learning guidelines.

 3.2 the media selections for instructional development and the instruction management plan for conducting the instruction

 3.3 the analysis of packages of any existing instruction that meets the given learning objectives

 3.4 the development of instruction for all earning objectives where existing materials are not available

 3.5 field tested and revised instructional materials

I think perhaps the hardest part of developing any new course is to figure out what needs to be taught. Now I know you're probably sitting there going "duh!" but I mean that on a deeper level. Too many times we jump to develop training only after a cursory look into the task being taught. What I've witnessed first hand, yes, from my own mistakes, is that what turns out to be the most important part of performing whatever task I'm trying to develop training for is something that is beneath the surface of what the "subject matter experts" tell me they do. If I also have had to do the task, it's a bit easier for me to validate, probe, and question, it gets much harder if I truly am an outsider trying to look in.

I'll give you an example. I was working on a course for Project Management. As I interviewed multiple successful Project Managers, all of them told me of the challenges of keeping the project on course through all of the individual tasks that had to be done in a specific order. We spent hours looking at PERT charts and GANTT charts, and even Critical Path charts. Once I had a fairly good idea of how to navigate a project through the paths, I started asking how they kept the whole project team to the timelines. That's when I discovered the heart of a successful project: communication! What these professionals do that distinguishes them from the average is that they all communicate regularly with the team. But that wasn't the heart of it yet! I talked with several Project Managers who all told me they communicate with their team. Several of them consistently had projects that failed. I realized that communication isn't the key component in and of itself. I moved on to the observation part of dissecting how people perform. Once I watched the successful people in action, and then compared them to those who struggled, the key component of communication came out. In both cases, everyone shared information with their team in both weekly live project team meetings (with some people on conference call phones) and weekly written updates. But what the successful Project Managers did was to go beyond that and communicate one-to-one with team members on a regular basis. It was this intimate level of communication that seemed to make the difference. We designed the training to include that element, the struggling Project Managers adopted the communication techniques, and their performance rose to the higher level.

While we're on the subject of project management, here's a freebie. While the communication was the key, it was a foundational element for another key PM technique: create and maintain a sense of timeliness from day one until the end. What caused many Project Managers to fail was what I'll label wasting too much time in the initial stages of the project because time did not seem that urgent. Later, when time was getting shorter, the pressure was greater, and so was the stress, and so was the resulting project failure. The good Project Managers knew that managing a project was really about managing the **people** of the project, not the tasks! They did things to keep moral high (communication techniques) and commitment to timeliness high (communication techniques.) If you want to know what those are, you'll have to take our Project Management course ...

The main thing I wanted to bring out with this discussion is the idea of **unconscious competency**. As you design and develop training, these are the key things you need to discover. What is it that successful people do that they're not aware they're doing? Those are the things you have to ferret out and build into your training design. You start by asking someone how they do something, and they'll tell you all of the things they can think of, and all those things matter, but the real differentiators are those things that they don't even realize they're doing!

How do you know when you're at the heart of the key skills, knowledge, or behaviors? When your subject matter experts say something like "Ah ha! I never thought about it that way, but you're right, I do have to … " The only way to get there is to keep challenging yourself and them to evaluate if you've looked at the task to be taught from every angle.

Let me suggest a magical line of questioning that has served me well through the years. After "What do you do?," and then after "How do you do that?," ask "What makes that possible?" Follow that closely with "Does that ever go wrong?" "Why?" Eventually you get to the heart of the matter.

To make it a little more scientific, because I know people love thinking of things when they're scientific, I guess because they seem so much more possible to master, here is a good series of steps to help you in the curriculum development process:

1. Identify your company's Top Performers
2. Ask the top performers:
   - What do you do?
   - How did you learn to do that?

3. WATCH the top performers
   - What do they do?
   - When do they do it?
   - When do they NOT do it?

4. Identify "hard to acquire" skills, knowledge, and/or behaviors
   - Resist the urge to train what's easy to develop training for

- Challenge the Top Performers 'status quo' understanding of what they are doing. They may not even realize it!

5. Design the training segment, with reusability in mind

Determining how instruction is to be packaged and presented to the student is accomplished through a media selection process, which takes into account such factors as learning category and guideline, media characteristics, training setting criteria, and costs. Instructional management plans (not the larger Management Plan, but the tactical level event management plan) are developed to allocate and manage all resources for conducting instruction. Instructional materials are selected or developed and tried out. All training events should go through a "pilot" stage where feedback is sought and initial adjustments are made prior to "release." When materials have been validated on the basis of empirical data obtained from groups of typical students, the course is ready for implementation. Development should incorporate elements that support the learning process (Gagne, Briggs, and Wager's Nine Stages!) to be followed in the next phase, Implementation.

Who To Use

On the subject of course development, let's spend a minute about working on multiple planes at one time, and talk about the use of business unit leaders and top performers. Now, being a Trainer for twenty years, I'm very used to "planes" that I have to get on and travel from one group to another, but these "planes" are planes of another sort ... We are of a profession that is tasked with, and hopefully gets intrinsic motivation, from helping others to grow in their abilities. Consider this, if you are working to develop a new course, then you certainly want to use the best subject matter experts you can get your hands on to learn how to perform the tasks you're trying to train against. However, if you also think of using those in the next tier out, then you accomplish two things at one time: you work on two planes at once!

When I say "the next tier out" I'm referring to those employees who are coming up in their ability and results, but who aren't yet in the top tier. Now it's an unfortunate by-product of modern business that those employees who have the right mindset (attitude) end up being busy beyond the scope of normal time and priority management. The result is a group of people who are consumed day-to-day with dodging lions and putting out forest fires. When the heat of the daily battle is at its hottest, and when it finally cools, there's little time or energy left for creative thinking. If you recall, we discussed earlier that a company's greatest need is to have employees who bring their passion to the workplace. The reason they need their employees' passion is that the passion brings creativity and creativity brings smarter ways to do the things they do to bring value to the marketplace. But then daily reality forces those who would be creative into a sort of "daily grind" just to keep up with the pace of the treadmill. Now you come into the picture! By involving the "next tier out" in the design and development of new course material, you invite them out of the daily grind and to draw aside into "out-of-the-box" mind stretching. Most often this element is one of the key ingredients to helping them reach the next level. It gets the "next tier out" to step briefly out of the grind and think through what they've unknowingly acquired as they've been working hard at their craft (remember our discussion about "unconscious competency"?) As they realize the depth of what they know, they start to bring that to bear during the heat of future battles. This is in addition to the practical ideas the group learns from one another!

I've found it particularly helpful to work with this "next tier out" as a group. Not that I'm advocating manipulation, but let's just agree to call this next ingredient I want to discuss "creative coaching." I recommend that you communicate with the "next tier out" group as a matter-of-fact necessity of developing a new course. As they interact around a specific project, you'll see them congeal as a peer group. And we all know what happens when talented people assemble as a group: they raise one another higher just by how they think and behave individually and interact as a peer group. While that may be your agenda all the time, and the specific course is a wonderful by-product of the more important goal, by letting your group know about it, you risk polluting the very waters that bring about the result you want. It will happen all by itself, just by creating the situation in which the group interacts, you won't have to stir the pot any more than simply mixing the ingredients together!

Creating Lesson Plans

For those who are like me and like lists and organized notes, the idea of a prepared lesson plan, (much like a script for a play or film) is a long-proven cornerstone in the education field. I find them essential to keep the learning event on track. A word of caution, though: while I am a stringent advocate of lesson plans, please keep the documentation details as brief as possible, yet thorough, so that the tail doesn't end up wagging the dog. I find that a detailed outline helps me more than a word-for-word script.

There are a lot of experts with a lot of variations on what should comprise the steps of the learning event and the contents of a good lesson plan. I started out using Gagne, Briggs, and Wager's 9 step approach, which is very good, but I've settled into an 8 step process for the learning event. I like to think of it more as the "flow" of the event than the "steps", because the key to success is **interaction** with the learners, and to maintain that I find I need a healthy dose of fluid motion not stilted regime. I do adhere to this step-by-step approach, though, because, as you do one step well, it makes the next step easier, for both the learner and the instructor!

When we talk about lesson plans, these are the functional level documents that help you make sure you have thought out what content the learning events will include, and how you will help others acquire it. A well thought through lesson plan is the best way to increase success in the heat of the learning event! Ahead of time, the lesson plan is thought out in terms of what will be needed for each of the steps that will be performed during the learning event. You plan first, document the plan, and then use the plan during delivery.

Lesson Plan Step 1: Grab ATTENTION and establish RELEVANCE

Think through ahead of time what will cause people to put into action what you plan to teach them. I suggest you inform them of the clear tie back to the money: the business results that will go up if the job task is done better. Document the key points of the payoff to the company and the people in your lesson plan.

Lesson Plan Step 2: Recall Prior Learning

Document the ties from past experience or learning that are the foundation or pre-requites for what you are planning to teach.

- **If** this is the next lesson in a series, tie the new task(s) to earlier tasks (builds upon other S,K,orB)
- Relate the task(s) to a common **work** experience that this is like. (analogy/comparison-contrast)
- Relate the task(s) to a common **life** experience that this is like. (analogy/comparison-contrast)

Lesson Plan Step 3: Pass New Information

Now we get to the heart of planning our learning: <u>**what**</u> we will tell people when it's time to pass new information. Lesson Plan step 3 is where we document the concepts and details that will be presented in the learning event. As mentioned above, I think the outline approach fits this need best. The question only remains as to what sort of outline to create . . .

Idea Mapping

Do you remember way back in Chapter Two I mentioned that there are strategic, tactical, and functional aspects to implementing Workforce Optimization theory? Well it's time to elaborate on a functional aspect of all of this Training strategies (engagement) and tactics (entertrainment). When it's time to actually get in front of a group and lead them through the first three steps in the lesson plan (and its execution) we DON'T WANT TO APPLY THE LESSON PLAN LIKE A ROBOT!!! There is a lot of planning of what ideas to introduce, and what pre-requites order to follow, but won't follow a set script to whatever degree that is possible. To keep from being to regimented when it's time to deliver, let me propose planning in your lesson plan an alternative structure: **Idea Mapping**.

Idea mapping means knowing the sequence in which concepts (and their skills) need to be introduced to a learner. If we were planning a day's learning event, these might become the items on a day's agenda. But once the sequence of concepts is established, within the functional discussion flow of each concept, prepare yourself to be able to move with the flow of your learner group's ideas.

You can do this by identifying the key points that comprise the concept, but don't force yourself or your audience into a regiment as to the order they will be learned. As something in one discussion triggers a nice transition to a new key point, move to that key point, or introduce it briefly, while building a bridge back to it for later. This lets your audience take smaller steps between each idea, as well as letting them have some control over the learning forum. You still manage the stops on the journey, but the group shares in the route taken to cover all of them.

To make this work to its fullest, you will also want to have multiple examples and illustrations ready for each of your key messages. Really, what you need to know is the key components that need to come out in the illustration, and then you can even create your illustration from something one of the learners says. For example, if I know I am discussing the key message that learning is really change, I know that I have to illustrate the fact that the change process, even when it goes well, requires extra effort. To make the point relevant, I can pull an experience from the group, but I need to remember that I need the example to have in it the element of added work. I might start by asking who has been through a recent change, get a volunteer to talk about it, and then I'll ask questions about what new tasks had to be done, what new processes had to be learned, what new people had to be met and connected with, and maybe what new computer systems had to be learned. It will be the learner's real-life experience that becomes the example/illustration to help convey the key message, but I have to know the core essential points thought out ahead of time in order to make sure, as we discuss the example in the learning event, the essential points come out in the discussion.

By the way, if they don't come out, you can always play it off lightly, and then bring it back with a statement about how they were lucky, most times change requires more work (to keep with our example/illustration.)

To maneuver through using idea mapping conversations during the learning forum, so you can avoid lectures, here are some preparation tips:
- Map out the pre-requites of all of the concepts.
- For each concept, identify the key messages.

- For each key message, prepare multiple examples and illustrations, but know the core points you need to illustrate.

How Much Information? Shorten the Journey

Have you ever noticed how people give directions to get somewhere? Some people start giving directions from the place where they're standing, and proceed to explain every twist and turn there is to the final destination. Those who are better at giving directions take the time to find out a mid-point that the person already knows how to get to, and then gives directions from there to the final destination. It's the same with the steps of learning. I like to think of it as people need a place to hang new information, sort of like hanging your coat on a coat rack. If there's no pegs on the rack, the coat ends up on the floor. I think we all know that illustrations and examples are great tools for increasing understanding and enabling retention and transfer, and the reason is that those illustration and examples help the learner to connect what you're telling them to something they already own, something they already know, something that's already part of them. You're taking them a few steps further.

This is the habit you'll need to cultivate in your training style. Take people from where they already are to each next step, don't start all the way at the beginning. You'll be surprised at how many intermediate places people already know about if you stop to ask. Stop and get a pulse from the group as to what their common experience is before you assume you need to start at the very beginning. Involve them in the learning by meeting them part way. Then, as you go, the illustrations and examples connect them to what they already know, and give them a place to hang the new stuff that you're introducing them to.

On a related note, but one that merits focus, is the topic of introducing new vocabulary. I've seen one popular approach is to explain all of the new terms first, and then, when the learner has the terms well in hand, use them to explain the pieces of whatever concept is being developed. I used this same technique early in my training development experience when I was working with some financial experts to build a course on Fair Lending practices. There were a few new laws that were driving the need for the training, and I had the brilliant idea of first explaining the new law, in order to drive relevance, and then to press on to how to change business practices to be in line with the new law. Great idea! The only problem was that, by the time the group finished learning about the new law they were so bored that they could hardly stay awake to learn the new techniques. I had yet to learn the first law of training: enterTRAINment – meet them where they are, not where you wish they were. It's not the job of the learner to bring their engagement to the course (although it would be nice!) it's the job of the trainer to create engagement, and without a good Training Designer building those elements into the course from the beginning, failure is imminent. And it was for my Fair Lending course . . .

Now I started this discussion talking about introducing new vocabulary terms but then hit you with an example of poor design of introducing a new law. Well the reason is that they're the same thing. Both are what I believe to be foundational elements to higher-level concepts, and I want to use them to warn you of a common training design trap. Just because something is foundational to understanding something else, don't be tempted to create a unit (or even a module) to address it upfront. Only introduce these things, (facts and terms) as they absolutely must be understood in order to enable understanding of the higher-level concept. As the need for understanding a fact or term arises in the course of teaching the higher-level concept, then introduce the fact or term AFTER you have developed the concept partially. Explain the meaning of the fact or term FIRST, and then tell them the word itself. Really, a "term" is only a label for an idea that makes it faster to communicate the idea by using the term for it. It's easier to assimilate a label for something once I understand the thing itself than to try to hold onto the label while I'm learning what it is. This training technique is known as "fact association."

Did you like that? Could you understand the term "fact association" better when it finally hit you in the context? What if I had started by telling you that "fact association" is a key element to learning and then went into what it was? You probably still could have understood it's meaning, but it's far easier when you bring someone around to the concept through the kitchen door rather than through the formal front entry hall door.

Lesson Plan Step 4: Demonstrate the New Task(s)

If they see the task done correctly they will grasp the new information you just passed more thoroughly, so you are going to need to **show** the learners how to do the task(s.) However, you need to show them in the most near-to-real-life setting as possible, (if task is to be tested, this is the same set of circumstances). Think about (and document) how, what, and where you can demonstrate the doing of the job task so that it is as close as possible to the real world as it can be without going into the workplace to do it. One idea for this is to think about what it is in the real world environment that will affect doing the job task differently than if it was done in a controlled environment (your learning event.) If "pressure to perform" is one element, them do the demonstration, the reinforcement (next step), and practices (the step after that) with a time test element. Even when time is not critical in the real world, it creates pressure, and that doing the task while under pressure is a critical element. Inviting co-workers or managers into the practice arena (step 6) can also create a "pressure" environment.

At any point, at step 4 in creating the lesson plan it's time to plan for how you will demonstrate the task, including how you will bring in these elements.

As you write your lesson plan, it will be helpful to document the demonstration details:

1. Demonstration Overview (describe the demonstration);
2. Demonstration Steps (list each step you will go through);
3. Demonstration Materials (list what you will need to do the task being demonstrated).

Lesson Plan Step 5: Reinforce the New Task(s)

Before building the task(s) into rote skills through practice, learners must do the task(s) accurately. Plan how the learners will demonstrate doing the job task while you are present to coach. Design your reinforcement (and the practices) to mirror a most near-to-real-life setting as possible, (if task is to be tested, this is the same set of circumstances.) It's not just practice that makes perfect, it's practicing it the right way that makes perfect.

Lesson Plan Step 6: Practice the New Task(s)

Once they know how to properly perform the task(s), learners need to repeat the task(s) until they can do the task(s) properly without having to think about the steps too much. Plan both the events of the practice and the time it will take into your lesson plan. Practice time is usually the first thing that gets tossed from the life boat when the event time is cut short, and yet it is the key to learning transfer (being able to do it right back in the real world.)

To keep things real, in a business environment, this is most often accomplished as class follow up. It actually creates a nice bridge from the mountain top training event back to the real world day to day perpetual doing of the job if you plan into your training design some element of "practice this when you get back to the work environment." This will require co-operation from the management team of the business unit, but is a practical way to apply what was taught in the training event.

The "practice" element, if done back on the job, should be designed to draw from work queues in the work environment, not just textbook examples that they do in addition to their real job. If the training event was to teach how to interview a job candidate, then have the post-class practice be to use a particular interview guide for the next ten candidates, and send a copy to the instructor. The instructor will then give feedback as though it were part of the training event. Why create busy work for either the learner or the instructor? This also builds nice interaction with the business unit managers! If the practice is being done while in the training event, then try to have the learners bring their work with them. I like to use the phrase "workshop" to describe this part of the training event, because, for some psychological reason, it makes people think that the training event was so worthless after all because they actually got something done.

You can even use the "bring your work with you" technique for soft skill training as well, if you think creatively in your design phase, and you prepare will for the event. Consider this, if we're learning how to interview, then reality tells us that there is some need to for the learner to interview people back in the real world (keep in mind, if there's no immediate use for the learning you shouldn't be teaching it to someone!) If you plan to have job candidates scheduled for the timeslot that corresponds to the "interview workshop" time on the class agenda, then, once they've tried the new task the right way and mastered it in the previous step, then the learner can actually practice the task(s) by interviewing real job candidates during the practice step of the training event. You're going to want them to use the new task skills, knowledge, and behaviors right away anyway, it may as well be during a step while you still have more control over insisting they use what they've just learned. On top of that, they'll actually be able to check off something on their "to do list" when they get back from the training event. Now you not only taught them something new, you even helped them get something off their pile that's waiting for them. What a hero you'll be!!

Lesson Plan Step 7: Check the New Task(s)

If you can write off the learning as successful, the learners have to be able to do the new task back in the real world. However, before you turn them loose, you need to make sure they can do the tasks in a controlled environment. Most often this is a mastery test, but it can also be a "juried execution of the task." One or more people can watch the learner do whatever it is that was taught, and then a score can be given. It's better to measure the right thing poorly (subjective grading on execution) than the wrong thing very well (a written test of fact regurgitation.)

Lesson Plan Step 8: Begin Transfer of Learning

This is where you plan the groundwork that needs to be in place for what will be expected when employees return from the mountaintop training event. The business unit leaders need to hold the employees accountable for actually doing their job tasks in the way taught, and also have some patience with them while they learn. What was learned in the training event needs to be **applied immediately**, or else learning transfer deteriorates. As the old saying goes: "use it or lose it!" There should be tolerance (and coaching!!) for those who are trying but not there yet, and no tolerance for those who would waste the company's investment by not applying what they just learned.

I've found planning the use of follow-up emails, with tips and even practice exercises helps to keep the flame burning. You may need to send follow-up emails to the business unit managers asking them to do specific things with the people they sent to the training event, and then send a coordinated email to the participants. Think creatively, but try to come up with excuses to stay in touch. Every little touch point helps to remind the employee of the mountain top learning, and that it was intended for them to use it to be more successful back in the workplace.

Once your lesson plan (or outline) is completed, it's time to get ready to put all this into action!

ISD Phase IV – Implementation

Implementation Phase Steps

    4.1 Implement management plan

    4.2 Conduct learning event(s)

Implementation Phase Outputs

    4.1 A completed cycle of instruction for the learning program

    4.2 Notes on time, space, student response, and success of materials; used to improve the program

There are two major parts of the Implementation Phase: enacting the management plan (pre & post event "stuff") and actually delivering the learning stimuli (usually a learning "event.") Business unit management should know what preparation their people need to complete prior to attending, and then be prepared to support them being away during the event, and also they should know (and do and/or oversee) the post-event follow-up. The forum of the learning event is a complicated mix of seriousness and light-heartedness. Learners must always know what is expected of them, and proven facilitation techniques will allow them to maximize the potential of a well designed course. Staff training is required for implementation of the instructional management plan and the instruction. The instructional staff must be trained to conduct the instruction and collect evaluative data on all of the instructional components. At the completion of each instructional cycle, training staff should be able to use the information to improve the instructional system.

Lesson Plans In Action

The second component in the Implementation Phase is to put our lesson plan into action: to convene the learning events. When you consider conducting a learning event, the most important thing you can do is to create the proper learning **forum**. I am referring to the atmosphere or environment in which someone is invited to participate as you enact your brilliant lesson plan. The degree to which you create a healthy learning forum is the degree to which your event will succeed, and your learners experience job impact success!

The Learning Forum

Author's Note – Get some fresh air, some sort of caffeineated drink, wake up, and pay close attention – this is a VERY important part of the kitchen sink!

The learning forum (the training environment) is the most important element of someone's learning journey that we're involved in (someone else will probably take the baton and run with it for the "coaching" part of the learner's journey to acquire ability). A large part of how much a person transfers from the formal learning event over to doing it on the job will be dependent on the level of their engagement during the formalized element. This is a different use of the word than the larger reference to "fully engaged" employees, although a more fully engaged employee will be a more engaged learner. What I'm referring to here is how much someone was able to pay attention and want to learn. There are things a professional will do that will heighten a learner's level of engagement.

When you think about training, think about it as helping someone "acquire ability." We'll talk more in a few pages about three ways that people learn (the pyramid), but now it's time to talk about the process whereby professional people help others "acquire ability." I had a great professor in my Masters Program,

Dr. Diane Lee, Ph.D. who likened being an Instructor to being a conductor on a train. The Conductor points out items of interest on the journey, and even frames them for the viewer, but it's the viewer who self-discovers the scene in their own mind. Without the Conductor the viewer may not have noticed, but the Conductor must never think that he or she can "make people see" they have to want to see for themselves. That's what a professional Trainer does.

What may not be obvious in this analogy, or maybe I just took it in a direction Dr. Lee hadn't intended, but I believe if I'm to think of myself as a Conductor on the journey, then I want to make sure I manage both the part of the journey I'm in charge of, and the parts before and after, by **removing any obstacle** from the journey that may inhibit someone from learning. So when we help someone discover new ideas and ways to do things, the most important way to help them is to first think about what would keep them from being able to learn, and then take steps to neutralize those elements. On a simple level, that means things like keeping the learning event free from interruptions. But a good Conductor wouldn't wait for an interruption to occur and then take action, no, a good conductor would cordon off the passenger car and put up a sign that no one is to enter the car while it is in motion. A good Conductor might even lock the door from the inside (we still need to be able to get out in case there's a fire!)

If you've been learning how I maneuver ideas into place, you probably recognize that all of that was my way of setting up this next point. I've found that one of the key elements to someone acquiring ability is how much they are able to pay attention during the formalized event. "Able" to pay attention may seem like an odd phrase for me to choose, but of course I chose it for a reason. I believe it is the instructor's job to help the person pay attention. Now they have to bring a certain level of interest, some of which can be stimulated by how well the event, and the skills or knowledge it is to impart, is positioned within job performance expectations, but once a person shows up with a reasonable willingness to listen, even if it's just a "let me see if this is worthwhile" willingness, then it's the instructor's job to know how to carry that initial attention willingness to the conclusion of the event. It's just a fact of reality that the level to which people are "plugged into" the experience is the level to which they'll retain what they experience. As engagement goes up, retention goes up. Retention is the primary element of job impact. There is only one goal of any training event, people leave able to do something better then when they came in, and it's our job to see that this happens at the end of the formal event, which all know is only the start of the learning journey.

And so, since engagement in the formal event is a key factor to everyone's success, let me suggest some ways to affect this all-important element:

"That's EnterTRAINment!!"

So what leads to engagement? Two factors: the forum and the content. It's self-evident that the content has to be relevant in order for someone to want to remember and apply it, but it's asking a lot for a person to be able to pay attention to a recitation of facts and figures, or even a demonstration. Remember, these are adult learners we're focused on, and these adults are probably over-tired from the hectic pace of modern life, and they also probably have a pile of work back at their desk that they'd rather be plowing through instead of coming to your training class. Well, maybe they'd rather be at your class, but they'd rather be at your class only if it's more worthwhile than the dent they would have put in their mountain of work by staying at their desk. So we need to meet these adult learners half way. While it may sound more than a little corny, I've started using a phrase that I think best describes the one element more than any other that I have found leads to engagement, it's the phrase "enter**train**ment". It's not just the passing on of facts, figures, ideas, and techniques that causes someone to remember them, a good learning experience should be enjoyable, and I'll even go so far as to say "entertaining". Hence, enter**train**ment.

By the way, I can't stand the politically correct label "facilitator" as though only a facilitator can stimulate learning. I'm even a little jaded at using the label "learner." If you're keen on these labels, or prefer some other, then feel free to cross out any other label I accidentally use and replace it with your favorite.

Anyway, back to the topic at hand, the facilitator of the learning event. There are two reasons why a learner learns from someone. Well, I guess there's really only one reason they learn and that's because the facilitator has something to teach, but I guess what I mean to highlight is that there are only two reasons why someone listens to someone in a training event, which is the first step to his/her learning something.

Reason #1 Why People Listen: The person speaking, of I meant to say "facilitating," has a high level of credibility on the subject. If the person in front of the group is a known expert, especially if there is a factual track record to substantiate it, people listen to them. It's a willing suspension of authority. It just seems like people are "wired" to subvert themselves to an authority figure when they come into a learning forum. If you think about it, they've already filtered themselves out as those who are willing to listen just by the very fact that they are present. UNLESS of course you are the company's internal trainer and you are convening a company mandated training class. Can you tell that I've been there? It was called "Total Quality" and there were the skeptics that REALLY didn't want to be there. I'll come back to that story in just a minute. I want to finish with this other point first. The key to using the "authority figure" is to actually know what you're talking about. People can smell a fake, but if you're genuine, then you'll already start out with a certain level of attention from your group. Use it well.

What works as a recipe for brining content experts into a training forum is also a great way to increase another important factor of training: transference (applying classroom training on the streets.) Management support is a key factor in getting people to want to learn. Having a job dependency be the skills and information taught in a learning event will heighten the learners desire to master the information, and hence higher attention, and thusly transference. If you create training courses that have built-in "cameo appearances" from managers and senior employees, not only do you heighten the credibility of the speaker, but you also heighten buy-in and support of management. Always a good thing! A cameo can be anything from a "fireside chat" at some point in the course, or even a module that he she leads.

The one requirement is that you make it easy for them to participate in the learning event. You'll need to have easy to follow lesson plans, with examples and illustration provided, but do not make these too scripted. Allow freedom for your managers within the pathway you define for the course. Let your "guest" enjoy helping others learn without the requirement of remembering too many complicated course elements.

There is a fine line you will need to manipulate, and I'd be misleading you if I didn't tell you about it. To get consistent involvement from seniors and mangers, you're going to need to let them feel like they're the cause of the success, which can sometimes be hard to accept. Not only that, the real pitfall is that these people might be prone to think that "training is easy, anyone can do it, you just get up and talk." To avoid this phenomena, you'll need to be very careful about how you explain the course from the start. Make sure they know that the course has an intricate design with deliberate stops on the journey, and that you, as the course designer, have mapped all of that out. I'd even share some of the psychology behind the lesson flow. Then make it clear that you are only asking them to participate in a small, but critical, part of the overall learning activity.

Regardless of the impression you may or may not create in the mind of the senior and/or manager as to the true competitive advantage training brings to a company, the goal you're really after is to heighten the retention level of your learners, and this will surely be accomplished as you involve these highly credible "cameo" appearances.

Now for the other element of retention . . .

Reason #2 Why People Listen: the person speaking is **engaging**. That sounds simple, but think about it in your own life. How long can you listen to someone who's boring? 15 minutes? 30 minutes? A full day class can seem more like torture than learning if the trainer is boring.

Before we go too far… what we're after here achieving a balance between serious content and gaining new ability, matched nicely with having fun. Who says training classes have to be boring? But, on the other hand, it's not comedy either!

And now for the rest of the story … as Paul Harvey would say,

I had been a corporate trainer for about a year, and had also learned some things about Total Quality principles, and so the company assigned me to develop and deliver a class on the subject. Everyone in the building had to attend. The first class went ok. About 24 people (there were 800 altogether, but I wanted to start small, just in case.) As the second class was starting, I saw two men in the group who I knew, had worked with in my previous department, and who I liked and respected. But they didn't want to be there. It took about an hour, but it soon became obvious they didn't want to be there. I should probably mention that it's not an option for a Trainer to fire people, or else I wouldn't have had the problems I did that day. Of course the company would have lost two good employees (they really were quire good at what they were hired to do) and that would have directly led to the company losing a Trainer, I'm sure. Anyway, the disruptive element of these two carrying on was more than a young Trainer like I was prepared to handle. I eventually had to declare a "coffee break" for the group, but asked the disruptive two to draw aside for a minute. Basically I asked them to bear with me and co-operate. I'm glad to say they did, but I'm at least honest enough to admit that it really had nothing to do with my "training skills" but rather our personal and previously existing friendship.

As I reflected on the day's events the evening, I was reminded of the first law of training I learned in Grad school (see, we have WO Maxims and now "laws of training.") To paraphrase: "if someone fails to learn in your class it's your fault." You can bet I wrestled with that too. How could it be my fault if those two guys didn't come there to learn? It was clearly their fault! No, it's still my fault. How? Well, it's my forum. It's that simple. They came into my world, and I either own that world or I don't. I realized that it is up to me to create the environment that brings everyone in.

A quick side note – there will always be that one person who challenges your forum, so you may still find you have to do the "let's all take a break – hey you, can we talk a minute?" routine.

Back to my out of control Total Quality class. Since I was a junior Trainer still, I did what most rookies do in a situation where they realize they have to achieve something but don't know how, I asked someone I thought would know how to take ownership of the forum. Here's their advice. Since the gentleman was named Mr. Norman, I refer to these pearls of wisdom as "Normanisms." So here's a Normanism for you. His advice to me was "if they want to be serious, you be serious, but if they want to have fun, you have fun." Guess what I learned? They always want to have fun! And why not? Think about it, a training class is a break from the routine! It's like a breather on the treadmill of business. And if we learn something as a result, well that's great!

So here's my advice about engagement and the element of "how engaging is the trainer?": be as entertaining as you can with your level of talent, and without taking it too far.

Oh, another side note – how you mix up "lecture" with "small groups" with "practice" will affect engagement as much or more than how enterTRAINing you are!

I guess what underlies this whole enterTRAINment approach is the attitude you will bring to your events. I will confess, I was taking things WAY too seriously. Maybe it's my German personality. I wasn't tapping into my ¼ Welsh creative roots! Whatever the cause, I was taking a "they need to learn this stuff so let's get down to it" approach, but the learners were definitely in a "I need a break" approach. Result? Train wreck. Ok, maybe I'm overplaying how bad it was, after all, I was a pretty successful Trainer in that regard, but I still will tell you I wasn't happy with the level of engagement of ALL the people in the groups.

Now, how can one be enterTRAINing? Ha! You got me! There's no way I can sort that out from here, (actually that's not true – if you'll read a few sections later you'll see some tips on creating an engaging learning forum – more so than just the "you" element) but I know one thing: if you never realize you need to be engaging you never will be! So I'd say the first step in becoming an engaging speaker is to always have that goal in mind. You will never have the luxury of being a boring speaker and expecting your audience to continue to pull themselves up by their ears and stay engaged. Well, I did have some tenured college Professors who seem to think that way, but then again, they were tenured, and it was college. We're not so lucky in the business world.

Maybe I'll see if there's any openings down the road at the University . . .

Ok, I thought about it some more, and I realized something I wanted to talk about was really part of this enterTRAINment point. Try to develop a habit of "talking in pictures." Good trainers use illustrations and analogies to help learners clue into the beginning of the concept. That's why I chose the "recipe" analogy for this book to try to explain the rather complex concept of Workforce Optimization. And since it is a really complex concept, I further brought in the "your growing a forest but tending to each tree" analogy. Talk in pictures. But not too many. Illustrations take people from a place they're comfortable with, because they either know it already or can grasp it quickly, and enables them to hang the new concept onto that starting peg.

So what's the moral to all of this? Try to be an expert, so you have Reason #1 working for you, and at a minimum, try to be engaging, so you have Reason #2 going for you. I've seen people listen for hours to a boring expert, or at least a non-engaging expert, but it really comes together when they bring in elements of engaging facilitation (yes, sometimes it's a necessary word to really make the point.)

Lesson Plan Step 1: Grab ATTENTION and establish RELEVANCE

Now that we've dispensed with the pre-requisite discussion about how to create the right environment for enacting your lesson plan, that leaves us to look at the actual conducting of the event as outlined in the steps of your lesson plan.

Start the learning event by clearly connecting the upcoming experience to their job success. You can show a slide with this, write it on the whiteboard, or pull it through interaction, but this is the starting point for what will become the most important part of any learning event: making sure it affects what gets done on the job when the event is over!
1. Tell learners what task(s) they are about to learn how to DO.
2. Tell learners when and how they will DO the task(s) IN THEIR JOB.
3. Tell learners how this way of performing the task(s) is the best way. (time/effort savings and/or increased impact)

Lesson Plan Step 2: Recall Prior Learning

You're trying to bring the group out of the jungle of the workplace and up to the mountaintop of the learning forum. People need to transition into a learning mode, even if the distraction is just the drive to the location the event is being held. If it occurs in the middle of the work day, the transition to learning is even more critical. To get people talking and tuned into what they're going to learn, you'll want to start them thinking about how they do the things they do now, and this will give the a starting point on which to build what you're about to lead them through. This is best done through interactive questioning.

- Ask how the task(s) to be taught tie to earlier tasks (builds upon other S,K,orB)
- Ask how the task(s) to be taught relate to a common **work** experience. (analogy/comparison-contrast)
- Ask how the task(s) to be taught to a common **life** experience that this is like. (analogy/comparison-contrast)

Lesson Plan Step 3: Pass New Information (Lead the Journey)

Once you have the group warmed up, tuned in, and forewarned as to what to expect, it's time for them to learn something new, after all, that's the purpose of a training event. Always remember, the reason people come to a learning event is to learn, and the reason they are coming to your learning event is to learn from you. That may seem like a stupid thing to have to say, but I've come across an increasing number of people who are taking the approach that they are only there to "facilitate learning" and their interpretation of that is that they will "pull" the information from the group, and that that group collectively knows everything that needs to be learned. I agree with this partly. I love the idea of involving the group, and I believe that the group knows most of what each individual needs to know, but to count on a group knowing everything, that's a little shaky. As well, a trainer should be able to rely on the course materials to carry the majority of the burden of credibility. But let's consider further this theory of training strategy that adult learners need to be **involved in the learning**.

For a short period of time I taught middle and high school students. Do you think they don't **need** to be involved in the learning? What makes this such a magic change once someone becomes an adult? I think it relies on the concept that adults don't like to "submit to someone" as though someone else is an expert and they're not. Once again, do you think that middle and high school students don't have the same **need**? If all you do is ask questions to let the group "self-learn" then you're ascribing to a methodology for failure. First of all, can you really suppose that everything is known by the group collectively? My experience tells me "no". My hunch is that your experience tells you "no" too. It's alright to "lecture" the group, that's what they're there for! They expect to encounter a "trainer," someone who knows something they don't. As well, I've seen too many instances where a strong personality will control the direction the group takes, and the person with the strong personality is just plain wrong.

Think back to a few pages ago when we looked at reasons people listen to others in these learning situations. The number one reason is the credibility of the speaker. Now, if there's someone in the group who is perceived (remember, reality is only one part of this, perception is what really matters) as "knowledgeable," then the group will tend to listen to him or her. If that person's approach is different in any way than what you have intended to instruct, and you're in one of these "pull the information" environments, then you have set up a confrontational situation where the group will eventually be forced to choose between you or the other "knowledgeable" person in the room, unless that person comes over to your perspective.

If you think about it from these multiple points of view, I think you'll concluded that at the heart of this "involvement/facilitation" theory is the concept of "engagement." People want to be engaged, interested, and challenged (actually, challenge is a component of engagement.) What they don't want is to sit in a lecture. No one wants to sit in a lecture, it's just that when we're younger we **have** to sit in a lecture. College students sit through "lectures" because that's what the college forum is – "lectures". But do you think we really do learn as much as we could in a lecture? If you've done any amount of training, you know that "lectures" are a luxury for the instructor and a chore for the learner. The learner carries most of the burden in a "lecture" based forum. They have to bring a higher level of interest in order to remain engaged, because the forum itself is one of disconnection: us and them, with a podium staged as the barrier.

Wait a minute, I just said a few paragraphs ago to feel free to lecture the group and now I'm saying they don't want to sit in a lecture?! Something's not adding up here!! That's why my first use of "lecture" (like that one) was in quotation marks! I'm trying to imply, like the last section of the recipe guide, that there should never be a boring, disengaged "lecture" environment, but rather an **interactive** "lecture" environment.

So how do we involve the learners without risking handing over the reins to small group "experts in the audience"? The balancing act is to _tell the new concepts (_push) but _pull examples, details, and application_ from the group. When you "pass new information" think of it as you will tell them the right way to perform **_a task_**, but then you will involve them by asking them to consider ways to apply what you're teaching. For example, in a course on interviewing, you might tell them to better assess a person's potential future performance, base your interview questions on past performance, so you need to ask situation/historical based questions, not hypothetical questions. That's the "new information" you're passing, a new way to look at interview questions. But then you'll ask them to take the hypothetical question of "_You have to work long hours in this job, are you ok with that_?" and turn it into a situation/historical based question (maybe "_Tell me about a situation where you had to work long hours and how you adjusted your personal time to accommodate the need?_") You've told them something new, it came from you, but they get to participate in creating the application of it. By the way, this is a good technique for interviewing, and is really powerful when coupled with "interviewing between the lines." For more on that, check out the section in this recipe book on the interviewing ingredient.

For some of the "new information" details, it's a good technique to use leading questions to let them "guess" what you're trying to explain. I like to make it light hearted by using the phrase "_that's right, we're playing 'guess what's on my mind' and we can't move on until you clear out the list that I have in my mind._" For example, if you're leading a discussion lecture on recruiting, and you want to make the point of looking for candidates with matching **behavior** sets not completely matched **skill** sets, and your point is that they exist but in different places than those the exactly match the job their recruiting for, then ask them where they might look for candidates that would have a similar **behavior** set (fyi – there's more on this recruiting technique in the section discussing the recruiting ingredient of our Workforce Optimization environment recipe). The "new information" you're passing is the concept of recruiting behavior sets not skill sets, and also that that opens up new recruiting pond options, but you'll pull the application as to what those ponds might be. Your leading question would be something like *"If we are looking for someone to work in a job in the Customer Service Department handling calls from irate customers, so they need to guard their reactions, what do you think would be a key behavior that we need to look for?"* From the leading phrases in your question the group will pick up on "tolerance" or "slow to anger" type of traits, and they'll guess something close enough that you can work it to the exact phrase you're looking for. I find phrases like *"yes, I'm leading the witness/jury"* and *"that's close, but I'd like to use the phrase _____, is that ok with you?"* help when trying to fine tune a group's responses.

You're trying to balance:
1. your telling of new information that they wouldn't know or guess with
2. their providing "content" through these guessing games, with
3. **helping them feel success**.

The feeling of success is an underlying need for someone to learn. It comes in later when they practice new skills, but it also comes in when passing new information.

Once you have the application "pulled" you can also pull examples to, once again, involve them without relying on them for the key new content. In our recruiting example, you could ask the group *"What are some possible ponds to go fishing for this even tempered candidate?"* The group will give you some ideas. If they're right, great, if you need to fine tune them, then use a phrase like *"Those are good. What do you think about _____? Do you thing that would be a good place to look?"*

The same "pull for examples, details, and applications" technique can be used when you're first asking about the behavior traits for this Customer Service person. Ask the group what they think are the essential behaviors of the person. Remember, you've already told them the key new concept of recruiting for behavior sets not skill sets, what you're doing now is **an involvement technique** without having to "involve" them in providing the initial key information. The group will get most of the items you're hoping for, and hence be involved, but then you'll guide them to fine tune and fill in the blanks.

Involve them in the training, and the byproduct is they will be involved in the learning, and learning transfer goes up. Of course you should practice enterTRAINment and make your "pushing" of the information interactive by asking for examples of when people found themselves in similar situations (not asking for how they resolved it) or telling engaging illustrations. Don't worry, the new information itself will drive relevance, and hence interest and retention, but you need to have some good "new information" to pass on.

> **Training Tip:** Our discussion of the "pull for examples, details, and application" involvement technique I hope has clued you in to the need to be prepared in advance with your lists. I like to use flipcharts to capture these group thoughts. I think it makes the learners realize all the more that their individual ideas/contributions are important to the training event when they see them written on a flipchart! To help me remember my list, I'll write my list ideas in very faint, small pencil notes on the flipchart. Then, as I go to write the group's ideas I can refresh myself on those I'm fishing for.

To maneuver through using idea mapping conversations during the learning forum, so you can avoid lectures, here are some preparation tips:

- During the event, you can draw from you "grab bag of illustrations" for the one closest to the group's discussion.
- Use whiteboards or flipcharts not prepared media (e.g., PowerPoint slides)

Explain in "Waves"

One more technique that I've seen really help people grasp new ideas is to use the approach to introduce the new ideas in pieces, a bit at a time, but at different times, which I call explaining in "waves." Hopefully you've seen this principle in action as you've been reading this book, and it's been working. We've already talked about using analogies, illustrations, and examples when you're explaining something to someone to help them relate, well this isn't that. Well, maybe it is, sort of. This concept is best explained by relating how it came to me: while I was at the beach – literally, not just symbolically. I was at a friend's house near the beach in California, and I decided to walk down and look at the ocean. As I was standing there, I noticed how waves reach the shore: they start further out coming from different angles, but, when they finally hit the beach, they hit the beach in the same direction. And they keep coming. Some stronger than others, but they keep coming. Eventually they wear everything down. Relentless pursuit. First the wave from the right hits, then the wave from the left, then from the right again, then from straight ahead, then from a 75 degree angle, neither left, nor right, but 75 degrees, then here comes the force from the right again, only this time with crashing force. Over and over until the ocean wins and the beach submits, and probably erodes too, if there's an Oceanographer in the audience who can set me straight on this.

As I stood there watching, it made me think of how people acquire knowledge, or better yet, how someone should help someone acquire knowledge. Now in the Training profession we're not about wearing people down, let alone eroding the beach, but I do like to compare it to the relentless pursuit of helping people acquire knowledge. **We should explain things in waves**. Give out a concept in small pieces, in many ways, from many angles, but always with the same target (the beach) in mind. Almost all concepts to be mastered require the acquisition of many small pieces of knowledge that get assimilated as the final understanding. The problem is that we have to introduce them to people in a linear order when they need to apply, understand, assimilate, and congeal them in a spatial manner. The best way to help them do this is to introduce things in waves. Give them one piece to a certain level, then give them another piece, perhaps to the same or a different level, then re-introduce the first piece to a deeper level, etc., etc. etc. It lets people begin to assimilate the pieces as a whole while they're gathering them together, and fully understanding one piece in focus at a time. It is far more effective (of greater impact and more efficient, hence it has an effect) than trying to plumb the full depths of one piece before moving on to plumb the full depths of another.

To master using this concept of explaining in waves, it's sort of like trying to become like that guy who used to appear on the Ed Sullivan show and spin all of the plates. To help someone grasp a concept with this technique, it's like starting one plate spinning, then starting the next, and maybe a third, but then returning to the first before you start a fourth, and so on. Eventually you have six or seven plates spinning and the learner is acquiring knowledge by leaps and bounds, but the teacher ends up exhausted. But fulfilled. Someone learned! Really learned! And that's what keeps us going after all, isn't it. Talk about "Motivational Fit!"

So there it is: "teach in waves." Don't be afraid to introduce one or two ideas into a learning experience. The phrase "that's enough of a glimmer on that for now, we'll come back and discuss that further in a few minutes. . ." will serve you very well to help people hold onto an idea until it appears on the next wave it's riding. People can handle multiple threads of a conversation, but don't forget you have plate number one spinning and not go back and either wrap it up or give it a few more twirls while you wrap up plate number four. People can even handle multiple analogies too. I hope.

Multiple People – Multiple Connections

Now for something that may be a bit painful, but that is critically important. Believe it or not, like it or not, you may not be the right person to train everyone. Hopefully that didn't hurt too much. Unfortunately, I have to go one step further in this brutal honesty if we're going to get the best forum for our learners. Even if you are the best person to train someone, at some point you may become "too much of a good thing." Where am I going with all of this? Just simply to introduce the idea of using multiple trainers in a class. The best match-up I've seen is to use a functional manager as the co-facilitator with someone who is a professional trainer. One person carries the burden for creating the environment primarily and bringing some worthwhile content, while the other elevates the credibility of the course, and hopefully can be somewhat engaging. Can you guess which player has which part?

Using a line manager has only one benefit to this multi-person forum, there are more reasons as to why I'm advocating you consider this for every class of which you're a part. Making the second trainer a manager is just one step better than a single trainer, because of the credibility factor it creates. The number one reason I like having two trainers is the connection factor people to people. Different personalities connect with different people. Ultimately you want all of the learners to be engaged in the learning, and who they "relate" to will be a factor in that connection. Having two people lead the training doubles the connection odds. The windfall to having the second person be someone from the management ranks is that it reinforces their support of the training back in the trenches. If they've been part of the training, it gives them better understanding of what was taught, and more buy-in to make sure it's used on the job. As well, if a manager has to invest the time to participate in training, then that person has a greater reason to make sure what is trained is something relevant to what needs to be done on the job.

As well, just having different "voices" and paces will bring variety to the event, and that will help to keep it a bit fresher, which will, in turn, raise the engagement level of the learners. Even the most engaging of trainers will eventually lull the class into repetitive listening, where they hear your voice but don't process all of what you say. When a new leader takes over for a module or two, the learner has to refocus in order to learn the new trainer's leadership patterns. You'll usually get through to the next person change long before repetitive listening sets in again.

Lastly, when one falls down, the other is there to pick him up. Now I don't mean that literally, but it's pretty close. When you're in the "hot seat" trying to lead a class, there's such a multitude of thoughts flying through your head at any given moment that it would take a real egotist to think that he can manage EVERYTHING. From time to time it helps for the second trainer to chime in from the sidelines. First it adds addition content to the discussion without the first trainer having to shove more ideas at people, but it also, once again, breaks up the flow. As the pair of trainers get more and more comfortable with each other, it really heightens the impact of the delivery to be able to jump off of each other throughout the day. I've even had people comment to me after a class that the fun he saw me and the second trainer having was the biggest reason he stayed focused. He didn't want to miss anything!

Now if you're not the "subject matter expert" and are worried about bringing someone in who might overshadow you, let me put your fears at ease. I've had the pleasure of being part of a training team with several strong personality managers, and every time it has been a success in both our eyes. What I typically find is that the new "trainer" is nervous about the event, and my "coaching" helps them through. Afterward there is a new appreciation for the skills needed to effectively lead a class. I'm not sure there's a better way to prove to the management team the value of having professional trainers in the organization! When the event is over and they get to experience firsthand the intrinsic reward of helping someone learn, the joy they feel is shared by you, and a real bond is created. I've always been careful to coach them gingerly on the skills of facilitation, keeping in mind that they are business unit managers and very influential in my career, but also that they will connect with the group in a way that I never will – through the credibility of the content! I may be better at crafting and managing the forum than they'll ever be, which I should be if I'm the professional trainer, but they will probably cause higher learning transfer due to the credibility factor of their being the subject matter expert. It's not important that they also be the most engaging trainer the group has ever met, the class will be a success as long as they're just a little bit engaging. If they're REALLY dry, then it's up to me to help supplement that from the sidelines throughout, and then coach on it privately as we go along. I've never had someone who resented my "training tips." In fact, it's always been just the opposite.

Lesson Plan Step 4: Demonstrate the New Task(s)

It's time, in the most near to real life setting as possible, (if task is to be tested, this is the same set of circumstances) to **show** the learners how you do the task(s). It's important to remind them of each technique you've talked about just as you're about to demonstrate it in front of them. I've also seen this demonstrate step work very effectively by having someone else, perhaps the co-facilitator we talked about having with you (remember an earlier section of this recipe book), come up in front of the group, and, as they go through demonstrating the new task, you stop them and comment on what the group should look for, what the demonstrator just did, and what the demonstrator will be doing next.

This "commentary as you see it demonstrated" technique works best when using co-facilitators because they can be prepped as to what to demonstrate and when you'll be commenting, but it also works to use one or two participants from the group. If you are going to use class participants, be careful! I suggest you choose them instead of asking for volunteers. Try to pick someone who looked like they were "getting it" while you were in "new information" mode. The last thing you want to have to deal with is someone doing the demonstration wrong! You'll have to correct what they're doing so that your class doesn't get wrong information, and that will possibly create a feeling of failure in the person who volunteered, and, even worse, a sense that "this is harder than I thought" in the minds of the learners. Both are barriers to learning transfer!

Effective demonstrations will need you to explain, before you start, the key elements of what is about to happen before the learners' eyes. Give them the overview of what you expect will happen, and also the steps you are about to perform. Once you've explained these, then you're ready to conduct the actual task demonstration.

Lesson Plan Step 5: Reinforce the New Task(s)

Have the learners do the task(s) while you provide input, guidance, and feedback. Let them do the task(s) one step at a time, with you reminding them of each thing they must do at each step. This is not "practicing" the skill, that's the next step, this is making sure they really can do the task in the first place. Next they'll practice it.

Most often there are too many people in the group for you to be able to give individual attention to each person as each person tries the task for the first time. To beat these practical time and space constraints, you may need to break people up into small groups, pairs, or trios for them to attempt doing the task for the first time. You can float around the room giving feedback, but the group by now will have a pretty good idea of what is needed, and can help one another try it out. This same approach can be used during the next step, practice.

Use pairs when the task is done individually, like driving a nail into a piece of wood (usually "hard skills" courses), but use trios when it's an interactive task, like interviewing a job candidate (interactive tasks are most common in "soft skills" courses.) The use of trios will let two people interact while a third can focus on watching, taking notes, and then providing feedback to the one attempting the new task. They can then rotate roles and do the exercise again.

The reason I wanted to give an idea of how to manage a group doing this reinforcing step is that this may be the most important part of the training event! Yes, you need to explain it the right way, that certainly is important, but it means nothing if they don't start to do it the right way when they return to the work environment! By taking the time in the training event for each person to do whatever it is that you're teaching, they will master the task more often, and hence have higher confidence levels that they can do the task in the new way, and hence do it that way more consistently when they leave the mountain top and go back to the real world. Don't be tempted to leave this step out of your training event just because it's hard for one person (or two) to tactically manage giving every person feedback. Think up ways to get the group to help you. You may need to create job aids (e.g., an "Observation Form") so people will know how to help you with this step, but you need to have the reinforce step in the training event.

Higher learning transfer, and hence training success, is dependent upon people having a chance to do the tasks being taught while you are there to give feedback. If nothing else, it's another way to check on step 7 . . .

Lesson Plan Step 6: Practice the New Task(s)

Let the learners practice doing the task(s). It's not just practice that makes perfect, it's practicing it the right way that makes perfect. As they practice it the right way, there will be little things that you'll help them adjust in order to get it perfect. Then make them do it the perfect way as many times as possible or as makes sense.

Lesson Plan Step 7: Check the New Task(s)

Since the overall course plan is to have learners demonstrate that they have acquired the S,K,&B by doing the task(s) that the lesson was intended to enable them to be able to do, now is the time that they do the task(s).

Lesson Plan Step 8: Begin Transfer of Learning

Ask questions of the group for how learners will do the task(s) when back on the job. Ask for ways to build self-accountability. Ask for ways to build accountability from others (managers AND peers.) By the way, remember in the Design Phase discussion I mentioned you should design in before, during, and after elements? If you didn't already have a serious discussion with the business unit leaders about the need for accountability and patience when employees return from the training event, then you've already shot yourself and your students in the foot at least, and maybe the head.

At this point, let the group know that you will be in touch, and that you'll send them "reminders, challengers, and more details" as you anticipate they'll be ready to apply them. Set the vision that learning continues after the event, and that you expect them to start using what they've learned so they won't lose it!

ISD Phase V – Evaluation (Control)

Evaluation Phase Steps

    5.1 Conduct internal learner satisfaction and skill tests

    5.2 Conduct validation of job performance impact and ROI impact

    5.3 Revise the learning program as needed.

Evaluation Phase Outputs

    5.1 data on instructional effectiveness

    5.2 data on job performance in the field

    5.3 a learning program revised on basis of empirical data

Evaluation and revision of the instruction are carried out by personnel who preferably are neither the instructional designers nor the managers of the course under study. The first activity (internal evaluation) is the analysis of learner performance in the course to determine instances of deficient or irrelevant instruction. Samples of internal validation are class surveys (level one data) and item tests (level two data.) The evaluation team then suggests solutions for the problems. In the external evaluation, personnel assess the job task performance on the job to determine the actual performance of course graduates and other job incumbents. Whenever possible, this should be a comparison of business relevant measurements taken on the individual before and after instructional intervention. Components of external validation, level three analysis determines if the instruction enabled the learner to perform his/her job duties more effectively; while level four analysis determines the impact of the increased abilities on the overall business metrics. All collected data, internal and external, can be used as quality control on instruction and as input for any revision of the system. Donald L. and James D. Kirkpatrick's book _Evaluating Training Programs: The Four Levels, Third Edition_ provides an in-depth understanding of this phase.

I think it is in the evaluation phase the P.E.R.F.O.R.M. really earns its keep! For the first time I am able to compare background and intervention to level 3 & 4 results!! This is the heart of the evaluation phase: "SO WHAT?!" If the intervention had no lasting effect on the output of the job function, then we shouldn't repeat it. If the intervention did have a lasting effect, then everyone who does anything related should experience the intervention too. It is the obligation of those who create and deliver development interventions to constantly challenge themselves and their handiwork to make sure it is serving the company at the highest possible level.

Challenge yourself to fly higher!!

Wrapping Up

Well, our recipe book is finally done! I know there were a lot of ingredients in there, and a lot of explanations as to how to mix them all together to create a delicious meal for your guests, even some time spent talking about how to serve your delicious meal. I think if we keep going with this analogy, there was probably even some time spent looking at how to clean up after the dinner party! It's all in there, and it's all part of creating a Workforce Optimization environment. If there's one final maxim I can put forth (I hope you're not tired of me by the end of all this!!) it would be: **HAVE FUN!!** If you enjoy what you do, others will enjoy it with you. If you enjoy it, you'll strive for higher and higher ground, and, as you grow in your professional savvy, your company will reap tremendous benefits.

Ok, one more maxim: just do it! While that sentiment make not be unique, it is what you'll need to launch your company's Workforce Optimization effort. I doubt that you'll be able to explain the concept well enough to get most management people tuned in to what you're trying to implement and achieve. The truth is that you're going to have to just starting doing it (remember the implementation steps!) and then they'll start to see the potential of what you are offering. If you wait for a big project support, it just won't happen. Take a deep breath, and just do it!

Now, while you're busy in the trenches, keep this thought clearly in focus: USE ME!! I'm here to help! If you look at music history you'll notice something interesting about human nature. In the 60's, America was experiencing "The British Invasion," where musical groups from England were becoming incredibly famous in America. Do you know what that was closely timed with? England was experiencing "The American Invasion!" Both countries were enamored of the music from the others' country! I see this played out still as I travel internationally and talk about what is going on in other countries. It's amazing to see how intently people listen when I tell them what someone in their field is doing in another country. It's like we're wired with an innate belief that someone else knows more than we do, so we'd better pay attention to what they're doing. You see the same human predisposition in companies who are constantly benchmarking their competition.

Now why would I insert this music history lesson so near to the end of our recipe book? If you'll indulge me a quote from my own personal hero, I think it'll bring it into focus:

> "A Prophet is not without honor except in his own country."
>
> — Jesus from Mark 6:4

Meaning, if you walk into the boardroom and declare you have arrived with Workforce Optimization in tow and demand a seat at the table, you're most likely to be booted right back out. Remember, there's no room at the trough unless we HAVE to make room (like for HR people who will advise us how to hire/fire without getting sued, we'll grudgingly give up a seat and a few scraps.) HOWEVER, if you let me help, and I come over to your place, and maybe bring some other HR professionals who have implemented Workforce Optimization, and TOGETHER we help your team see the benefits, then you'll stand a better chance of getting an invitation to sit down and eat some of the feast you've helped to prepare! No guarantees. But at least it's a better bet! I'm here – use me!! The chances are pretty good that I won't even cost you anything. Now how can you beat that?!

Workforce Optimization is a science, but the success lies in the art of applying the science! **May you enjoy ever-increasing success and fulfillment as you become a master chef!**

Please feel free to contact me (www.RSMSOL.com) as you travel on your journey!!

Appendix One:
The Recipe

If you turned here before reading the book, I'm not sure whether to say "you're smart" or to say "go back to the beginning." I thought I should provide as definitive of a list as possible of all of the elements that go into a Workforce Optimization environment. These are the pieces of the puzzle of which I think one has to be aware and manage if you seek to create the right environment to foster maximum employee job performance. Here we go... keep in mind that each bullet item has a world of depth behind it!!

- Company goals and initiatives
- Organization job structure and inter-relation
- Customer satisfaction measurements and enablement strategies and techniques
- Organization-wide communication plan
- Job definition (process, job tasks, outputs, and measurements)
- "What job performance should be" analysis strategies and techniques
- Career planning and internal promotion strategies and techniques
- Recruiting, Interviewing, Hiring, and Termination strategies and techniques
- Skill and Knowledge acquisition plans
- Behavior alteration plans
- Employee Accountability strategies and techniques
- Employee job performance coaching strategies and techniques
- Rewards and punishments strategies and techniques
- Systems and tools to enable Workforce Optimization
- Change Management

Appendix Two:
Implementation Steps

Is there a right or wrong way to implement? Well, in a word, yes. I think the best way to bring about change is to fly under the radarscope until you've built enough of a successful track record that people can see and evaluate, from their world results, that what you're talking about is valid. With that in mind, I offer these steps for implementing Workforce Optimization at your company:

1. Define company goals, business units, & performance metrics.
2. Contact Ken to discuss.
3. Define jobs: job tasks, and task skills, knowledge, and behaviors.
4. Contact Ken to discuss.
5. Develop training courses for job task s/k/b's.
6. Contact Ken to discuss (Get the idea? I'm here to help!)
7. Supervisors learn and use coaching for performance.
8. Employees use Best Practice's for self-learning.
9. Offer courses for job task development.
10. Employees learn and use Career Planning for self-assessment.
11. Workforce Optimization Analyst uses comparison tools to identify performance-enhancing factors.
12. Contact Ken to discuss (I couldn't resist that one more time!)

Appendix Three:
What Matters

While you need all of the elements, some are more mission critical than others. This chart is an attempt to help guide you in setting priorities as you create your learning environment.

What	Rank
Management Plan	50
Tie to Business	45
Learning Environment	25
Engaging Learning Events	15

Appendix Four:
Workforce Optimization Maxims

Maxim #1: The purpose of Workforce Optimization is to maximize business results.

Maxim #2: Never add work in order to measure work.

Maxim #3: Always keep the big picture in view.

Maxim #4: If it affects job performance, I need to understand it!

Maxim #5: Consider what peer groups exist that could affect results and check them.

Maxim #6: Focus on <u>behaviors</u> when you go fishing.

Maxim #7: Past performance is not just the best way to predict future performance, it's the <u>ONLY</u> way to predict future performance.

Maxim #8: People learn quickly, but people change slowly!

Maxim #9: You can't "train" chaos.

Appendix Five:
References

Louis Carter, W. Warner Burke, Edward E. Lawler III, Beverly L. Kaye, Jay Alden Conger, John Sullivan, David Giber (Editor), and Marshall Goldsmith (Editor), forward by Richard F. Beckhard (2001), *Best Practices in Organization Development and Change: Culture, Leadership, Retention, Performance, Coaching*, San Francisco, CA: Jossey/Bass Pfeiffer, ISBN 0-7879-5666-X

Kirkpatrick, Donald L. and James D. (2006), *Evaluating Training Programs: The Four Levels, Third Edition*, San Francisco, CA: Berrett Koehler Publishers, Inc., ISBN-10: 1-57675-348-4; ISBN-13:978-1-57675-348-4

Robert M. Gagne, Leslie J. Briggs, and Walter W. Wager (2004), *Principles Of Instructional Design, Fourth Edition*, Belmont, CA: Wadsworth/Thompson Learning, ISBN 0-03-034757-2 (First Edition 1992)

Robert F. Mager and Peter Pipe (1997), *Analyzing Performance Problems, Third Edition*, Atlanta, GA: The Center For Performance Improvement, Inc., ISBN 1-879-618-17-6 (previously ISBN 1-56103-336-7) (First Edition 1983)

Appendix Six:

Securing Your Copy of
P.E.R.F.O.R.M.

With your purchase of "*All These People*," you are entitled to a free personal-user copy of the proprietary P.E.R.F.O.R.M. software from RSM Solutions, which will support your implementing workforce optimization.

To get your free copy of P.E.R.F.O.R.M., all you need to do is to log onto the RSM Solutions website, www.RSMSOL.com, and look for the **Downloads** link in any of the menus.

On the Downloads page, you'll see step-by-step instructions for downloading the files which comprise the P.E.R.F.O.R.M. application suite.

If you have any questions at any time about how to use P.E.R.F.O.R.M. or how to secure your copy, please email me at Inquiry@RSMSOL.com.

I wish you all the best, and remember, I'm here to help, so feel free to contact me!

Made in the USA
Middletown, DE
07 May 2016